LOVING MUMMY

ISBN 978-0-244-73827-3

Acknowledgments

To my family I want to give a big shout out for the continuous source of inspiration I could never have gone through life without. My life's journey you are a part of, chosen for your special thing, I am blessed to have you in my life to me you mean everything.

To my children I love you so, you taught me my biggest lessons in life on how to grow. You matured my heart with patience and strengthened my soul, without you I would be lost. Courage, wisdom and understanding is what you have brought out of me, I am honored to be your mummy.

Thank you to my friends particularly Shanie, Kim and Allison you are my rock, in times when I could not hold myself together you never let me drop. My spiritual sisters who has walked along side me many a path, I have great love and gratitude for you for without your support many things would never have come to pass.

To the corner stone of my being, the beat of my heart, I want to say thank you mother dearest for all your teachings of love that never fell short off the mark. Without your lessons of living I would never have known how to fly, thank you for having me to experience, what is life?

To life itself with all its hidden mysteries of how it all began, thank you my Almighty Father for always extending out your hand, when many a time I have placed myself upon a barren land. The light you shine makes a dark passage clear and safe to walk home, in you I am alive, through you I am revived, with you I am never alone.

Filled with Loving Memories

My Brother
30th June 1969 - 30th September 1990

R.I.P Grandad 1929 -2009

In life, you were my rock and in death you are my haven. When I feel and think of you, I draw upon strengths that keep alive your memories in me. I share the highs and lows, lessons and teachings of knowing and loving you with the hearts and mind able to listen, so that your death becomes a rebirth and from that rebirth comes forward new life. Your name lives on forever in me. Sealed with a loving kiss, I love you Nicky

Introduction

As a young girl growing up in the heart of Hackney, I would often dream of writing my story down of living with a mum with mental health and share it with whomever would want to listen in the hope, that if anyone was in my position they would not feel as alone as I once did. Driven by circumstances that change like the wind, entwined with spirituality and strange goings on, I am compelled to open my heart and release its contents.

Putting pen to paper placed me upon a reflective path, a mental, spiritual shuttle service and through this amazing journey, I have battled with demons and been guided by angels. I have closed doors that were left ajar and opened windows that were nailed shut. What was once a dark and lonely place has slowly begun to be filled with light.

Guided by, "Be true to myself," my mind, body and soul has undergone a spring clean that has had me in fits of laughter one minute then reduced to tears the next. A roller coaster ride, it has been. Sending me down a path that has allowed wounds of old, left unattended for far too long to finally begin to heal and equipped me with tools of recovery for future journeys to come.

All new chapters start with a blank page upon which we transcribe our minds eye. As a blank canvas is placed before me to create the picture of my own future, I give myself permission to step into the place of vulnerabilities and the unknown and not be afraid.

Moment of Thoughts

It's quite hard to know where or how to begin when consumed with a multitude of thoughts and emotions obscured by truths, I somehow knew existed but had yet to truly discover. Embarking upon a voyage searching the very fabric of my soul to discover who I really am, my life has gradually unfolded like stumbling upon an old chest in an attic. Instinctively I sweep away the cobwebs and matter which have lain dormant for many years and pinch my nose at the fowl stench it gives off. As I cough, and choke overwhelmed with dust, I persevere to see the hidden treasures. Slowly pealing back, the layers of forgotten time where both sadness and elation resides, the unexplainable begins to reveal answers as I learn about myself in reverse.

My life seemingly written by many hands before my birth, I find myself walking a path that once was mine, collecting all the sorrows and tears left behind. Thrown into a gust of wind spiraling beyond the understanding of self, my consciousness searches for a higher discernment. I never tire of wondering, What if? What if things had been different, would I have been the same? If I had not served my life lessons, would I have been able to appreciate the values of its teachings?

Discarded in its hiding place many questions remain unanswered, just like in the attic of my mind. Never the less I am reminded by life natural healer, I cannot run neither hide from my past, present or future no matter how deep it is. I am urged to awake and experience the day.

As I reach out, I pray that someone will see hope to be inspired to seek and understand thyself, better. I pray let there be one rather than none, that sees they are not alone in life forever spin cycle and that they truly ascend from great courage and strength. The woman in me has stirred. I believe it's time for me to wake up.

Ten Years Old

Here I am searching for clues as to, "Why me?" Slowly but surely, I begin to unlock my forgotten memories long since buried. Seeing with my waking eye I breathe life into unearthed secrets as I am brought back to the age of ten.

The beginning had happened a long time before I worked out that something had begun. I was already living in the end of something familiar and once loved. I was beginning something new that would evoke immense sadness and mystery of which I had never felt before. I didn't realize that our family joy was being stalked and harnessed with the soul intention to remove the foundations upon which we stood with one swift blow. I thought all that, "My experience changed my life stuff," only happened in films, never to people we knew, never to us and not in Hackney. Why couldn't we have won the pools? Now someone always wins the pools.

Growing up I was oblivious to the harsher side of life. Enjoying living under the shelter and protection of mum I was so inquisitive with a thirst for greater understanding forever questioning why? So, I could conjure up ways to make my life that little bit easier. I was comfortable in my own skin and could play alone entertaining myself for hours.

Being the youngest of three I sat in the seat of observer and learnt quickly how to remedy the mistakes of my brother Nicky and sister Cecile. Basically, do well at school, do as I am told at home and I will receive rewards, it was as simple as that. This meant being given freedom with trust to do my own thing but more importantly being able to go places with mum, a privilege my brother and sister rarely got. As far as I was concerned, I was in a powerful position, I had all that I needed, nice clothes, plenty toys, my family and the very beat of my heart, MY MUM.

Mum was born in Jamaica. She was the third oldest child out of six. Her father passed away when she was a young girl and her mother my grandmother Mama Sarah remarried to a Mr. Clayman, resettling in England during the midst of the wind rush movement. As common practice at that time parents came over first then sent for their children when they were properly settled in. Mum would have been a young teen when she first touched British soil.

Of the little I know, life was far from plain sailing for her. Her mother no more than four feet and a bit tall was a dominant force who ruled the roost inside and out. She was the lantern of which everything orbited. I always got the sense that her and my mother's relationship was slightly estranged as there didn't appear to be an open bond of affection between them. I was of the impression that mum was closer to her father and that her relationship with her mother had always been that way. Mama Sarah adored Cecile, liked Nicky but never really took to me. Don't get me wrong I have plenty memories of her saying hello but none of those lingering hugs you get.

With intangible rifts to mend mum walked many a terrain of hardship and suffering often having to fight the elements alone, but a fighter she was. Come the early1980s things started to look up for mum. She had plans to set up her own clothes business and buy a car. Mum had a determination about her that when she set out to do something those who dared get in her way were soon bold over for example, at the same time she was making plans to upgrade her family, she was also secretly planning to wed her long-term boyfriend Ronnie, whom she had been with since the early 1970s. We found that out on the day of her wedding.

Mum decided she wanted to move the family from our small three-bedroom flat into a massive three-bedroom house. I felt sad because I liked living in a block of flats. It was my extended family where everybody knew you and your business but watched your back at the same time. I had so many fond memories of exploring derelict buildings, penny for the guy and playing the un-tiring game of knock down ginger. I was aware that I would be starting all over again from knowing everyone to knowing no one.

However, when mum took us to view the new house, I fell in love immediately. This was the biggest three-bedroom house I had ever clapped eyes on. All I could see was a massive red front door, the kind of door you might see in a school and when you open it, for a moment, your breath is taken away by the share volume of the passage.

I remember looking at the ceiling and thinking, look how high it is, with its beautifully decorated designs, only my grandmother's house could compare to this and that was twice the size of our new house. The kitchen was huge, the sitting room was even bigger, and the bedrooms were at least twice the size of the rooms in our old flat. With four landings and everlasting steps, this wondrous house also came with a garden, our own personal playground that seemed to stretch for miles.

The house enchanted us all and the only decision to be made was when were we going to move in. Mother wasted no time in reflecting her turn of fortune in our new home. With her plush ways, unique dress sense and flamboyant life style, no expense was spared when it came to surrounding herself with luxury. Without saying, the house had to be kept immaculate. With varnished floorboards covered with sheepskin rugs, we had a top of the range TV, an eight-seated solid oak dining table, a cat that I found as a kitten and named Tabby and a dog named Dusty from Dusty in the series Dallas which mum bought. However, the final seal of approval for me was the new school my brother and I had changed to. We were now going to Northwold, which we were both happy about.

Everyone seemed to settle in relatively quickly. Cecile and I were still having the same arguments as to whose side of the room belonged to whom. Nicky had his own room so for the first time he had to clean up his own mess. I was up to my old tricks discovering all the hide out spots, like the storage space above the bathroom where I would often play with my dolls and hide from doing the dishes.

Summer time the garden would become my brother's and I retreat. We would make mud pies, catch flies and wasps in jar and watch them fight, as you do when you're ten. We would often go digging for treasure and even though all we ever found was bits of lead and broken glass, it always felt like a victorious moment.

To boot, the street we lived on was great too. It was the kind of street that seemed quiet at first glance, but if you stopped and allowed yourself to be still for just a moment, you begin to realize there's a lot more going on than meets the eye. It ranged from the all weekend party throwers, to wives throwing out husbands, couples having domestics and children running riot. It wasn't that different from living in a block of flats after all and as for making friends, that seemed to occur over night.

Falling back into a family routine was an easy transition to say the least. I was running up and down with mum, meeting many of her eccentric wealthy friends who ate in fancy restaurants and lived in fancy houses somewhere in the abyss of, "No place I have ever been before." They all had children who were roughly my age too and who equally were eccentric in their ways. We would go for walks in the countryside, stayed in caravans and go horse riding. For those short moments, I was loving my life and the perks it came with.

Everything seemed to be going great, it was the beginning of something new that I wanted to last for forever. Ronnie was attempting to hold down a job, he never really was a morning person and mum was being mum as always. Happy is to a simple word to describe the joy I felt for the family I had been blessed with, for our new home, new school, new friends and new dad who I loved and adored.

For one year my real-life Eden blessed me in abundance until tragedy struck the house. Tabby had swallowed a fish bone in the night, unbeknown to me at the time the bone had pierced his lung which was making it difficult for him to breath. I recall waking from my sleep to sounds of faint coughing. I crept down the stairs to find Tabby coughing, trying to clear his throat. I rubbed his neck, repeating, "What's wrong?" Concerned, I woke up mum and told her that something was wrong with Tabby. She told me not to worry and sent me back to bed. In the morning as we all prepared ourselves for school, mum said that she had taken Tabby down to the vet during the night, but everything was going to be alright.

I had never contemplated death being involved in my equation of life. I didn't even know what death was, how it felt or more importantly what it meant. I had never thought about it before. Subconsciously unaware of my distress of Tabby being in pet hospital, I behaved extremely bad at school that day. I threw a chair at Mr. Hardin the Scottish Science Teacher. I cussed, cursed, and beat up one of the girls in my class for making racist remarks to me.

The school phoned home immediately informing my parents of my behavior. There was no catching the mail in the post for me this time, Mr. Hardin made sure of that. He was so smug and always threatened me with phoning home there on after as if to say, "I know black kids get beats," and he wasn't wrong. I confess my thoughts could only penetrate on what I thought soon to be my wake. The distress of my beloved Tabby stuck in pet hospital had evaporated from my mind.

Mum was no push over when it came to dishing up discipline to her children and by that, I mean licks. There was something very menacing and physiological in her need to prolong your suffering. She'd meticulously prepared you for the inevitably and the longer the talk, the harsher the punishment. She had a trick of making you feel so relaxed when giving you an explanation of what you've done, what you were going to get and why, you'd fool yourself into believing she's going to change her mind and let you off with a warning. With your guard down and not properly reading the mummy stare that's letting you know this is a deadly serious moment, she'd hit you with a low blow and utter the words that all black children who knows fears, "Go and get the belt." I knew today was going to be a long, long talk and I was afraid.

When I arrived home, I went straight into the sitting room where I knew mum and Ronnie would be waiting for me. Sure enough, there they were sitting side by side on the settee in an upright position with a facial expression I had never seen before, it was too calm. There was about a five minutes silence of me looking at them and them looking at me when suddenly, mum's mouth begins to open in what appears slow motion, upon which I instantaneously synchronize into a physical, mental meltdown when I hear the words uttered, "Tabby's dead."

Wide eyed, tears consumed me. It was then it dawned upon me what death meant and looked like. To be left at any time, without warning, never to have again, being lost in the wilderness just like Lassie. Half the time I couldn't watch a full episode as it always made me feel depressed. I yelled, "No," as I ran to my room, flinging myself on my bed, weeping and wailing uncontrollably. What was I going to do without my beloved cat that was my friend but more importantly a member of the family?

I must have wept for hours when out of nowhere a thought entered my mind. I sat up on my bed, wiped my eyes and started to smile because something amazing had occurred to me during the midst of my grief. This beautiful cat I had found as a kitten, which I named Tabby had served me one last good deed for which I will remain internally grateful. He saved me from a serious ass whooping. Only God knows what I would have got that day for my unacceptable behavior at school.

From that prospective, death didn't seem so bad for I had been saved from receiving, "Ten of the best," as mother would say. Naturally I played at being sad for as long as I could milk it hence receiving loads of hugs and kisses. For a few weeks after, the house was in a state of mourning but secretly when I was alone, I would smile to myself with thoughts of what finding him had brought and done for me and the good memories he had left behind. Little did I know that those feelings of loss, never to have again would soon feature big in my life.

After the death of Tabby, our lives as a family took a dramatic turn for the worst. There were no more happy times. What I once knew and remembered had been cut short and no longer existed. All of what was clear became vivid and all that was strong and solid began to fray and crumble. Our new home and family began to resemble something unrecognizable, unidentifiable and unexplainable to me. Indeed, a flying object had landed in the core of my home rocking the very foundation upon which I stood.

Nicky was sent to boarding school living what I saw to be an independent life. My sister was on the verge of leaving home anytime soon and mixing with the wrong sort if you know what I mean. Ronnie had moved out the house, the marriage had broken down beyond redemption and seemingly so had my mum. That's when it became apparent to me just how much of mother's life revolved around keeping Ronnie.

The further her marriage sunk to depths of no return, the harder she tried to keep it afloat. There was nothing that she would not have done for him. The only problem was, Ronnie was not as motivated as mum, he was more the laid-back type. My brother and sister nicked named him eat, sleep and watch TV. Besides, he had no reason to work as mother was the breadwinner, the care taker and she made sure that everyone had what they needed, until the day he left her for another woman.

From that moment on I am sure mum's heart stop beating. She tried desperately to keep herself together but eventually, the paper covered cracks turned into gaping big holes and what was once incognito gleamed like stars. Mother was no longer the breadwinner, the hard worker, the fighter who always strived for the best for her and her family. She was becoming the blinded crier who swallowed the pill of betrayal and rejection daily, rendering herself powerless to see the world beyond herself. Mum was on a journey. It was later that I learned that this journey that takes you to places of different dimensions, that can evoke intense extremities of expressions and behaviors the like of which I had never known or seen before and something mum was no stranger to, was a place called depression.

There was nothing and no one who could save me from this horrible truth being thrown in my face like no custard tart I had ever known. It contained rocks, bits of broken glass and anything blunt or sharp that could cause serious damage. The worst thing of all, the thing that sealed the confusion and chaos, was the fact that mummy was doing all the throwing. The beat of my heart, the reason for living, all of what I wanted to be had become the attacker and no longer the giver or soft place to fall.

What I once felt did not matter or have care for as a child, was about to become vital lessons to my survival. I remember asking myself for the longest time, "How, when and why did this all happen?" Maybe I could have done something different to stop it all. Everything seemed to happen so fast whilst little old innocent me, nearly thirteen and still playing with dolls heads had to become, in adult terminology, "Responsible." What did I know about responsibility? I was just a child and that's was the way I liked it and wanted to keep it.

Nothing could have prepared me for the life journey I was about to take. I spent a lot of time kicking and screaming, denying and avoiding, pretending and hiding what I knew I would ultimately have to face. Unavoidably, that day came when I least expected it and just like a bee sting, it flippin' hurt and left me in shock for quite some time.

Thirteen Years Old

There was no longer sister to ask what to do, not even to fight with anymore. Cecile left home soon after my thirteenth birthday and shacked up with any mother's worst nightmare. Her life was fraught with difficulties drugs and violence. I would have loved her to be able to help me, but I knew she had enough problems of her own to deal with. Then there was Nicky. Like my sister, he had reached maturity age and doing his own thing. I seldom saw him at home, and we didn't seem to talk as much as I remember when we were kids. He was in avoidance just like my sister about what was happening to mum and to fill the void of, "The good old times," he strived for so many things one of them being to be a force to be reckoned with, a bit like mum. His nickname was Scrapes on the streets.

I too wanted to be absorbed with stuff that took me away from the here and now, but there was no one beneath me to pass the buck to. Everything got laid at my feet. I had nowhere to go, no form of income and no qualifications in life skills, I hadn't even started my period. I was frustrated and resentful that circumstance had nominated me, "The one," that everyone comes to when things go wrong. I wanted to be the child I remembered I was, not someone who pretended at being the child they used to be. I yearned for that family feeling of togetherness as if pre-disposed to a permanent thirst. Unfortunately, it only served as a torment to my already weary soul for whilst I could block out my reality in my head, my eyes could not help but see what was manifesting before me.

One night as I sat on my bed relaxing, I was distracted by a subtle sound of weeping coming from the room next door, mother's room. Not sure what to do and slightly taken aback having never really heard my mother cry before, I hesitated and thought for a while. I kept seeing myself as a little girl no more than five years old in care home with a gash above my right eye where the carer had hit me with a whip. The whys and therefore surpass me but I knew mum was coming to visit me that day. I kept noticing how dry and white my skin looked and how knotty my hair was. I don't remember leaving, I just remember seeing mum, mum seeing me and then being back at home.

As I was brought back to the sounds of mother's cries, it was then I knew that whatever had to be done concerning my mum, was going to have to be done by me. I deleted the word, "Options," from my mental and emotional vocabulary and replaced it with, "Shit happens." I was not about to abandon my mother in her time of need. No amount of stuff could stop me from returning the love to the one who gave me life.

With a gallant heart, I arose from my bed with the intention to put my arms around her and tell her that everything was going to be alright. However, as I reached her bedroom door, I froze and just stood there looking at her crouched by her bedside weeping into her chest with despair. I was afraid, afraid that I had never seen her looking so weak. This was not a case of do something good to please her and then she'll forget her troubles and reward me with a gift. This was more serious than I could have foreseen and was going to take a little more thought.

Lost in contemplation, I could see mother was oblivious to my presence standing at the foot of her bedroom door. Suddenly she looked up at me in fright. Her face read, "Help me Shavon," which quickly turned into hysterical laughter. Her eyes where so squinted with laughter I wasn't sure she could even see. As I looked on in total disbelief my body began to tremble with fear. The metamorphosis from sane to insane happened within a blink of an eye. Paralyzed to where I stood, I attempted a measly, "Please stop, your scaring me," but I don't think she heard me. Her eyes seemed empty or focused. They possessed a wild glaze that didn't look at you, but rather through you.

My brother on this occasion was at home changing to go out. Upon mum's high-pitched laughter he came rushing out of his room to see me locked in trance at mum's hysteria on the floor. He quickly pulled me back into my bedroom as he kept saying, "Stop it mummy, can't you see your upsetting Shavon." I don't remember my brother leaving the house that night or the sound of mother's laughter stopping. I just remember sitting on my bed as if I had sat in the same spot for days but only, I knew it. This was an experience I was to become a frequent visitor of.

As if at war, I was suffering from shell shock. Time in the real world often stood still propelling me into an abyss of visions of the past, present and the future. No frills or pleats could disguise the unthinkable truth of what is which was, as much as I loved my mum and clearly sensed her anguish of breaking up with Ronnie, she was losing it.

It would seem like days, but I know it was months when mother decided to kick Nicky out the house. Leading up to that day there were a series of events that took place. The first was when my brother and I did something in the house of which we knew nothing about. We tried to contact the dead. I saw some girls doing the Ojai board in school and wanted to try it. I wanted to speak to my uncle Troy whose life was taken a day after his birthday and whom I missed terribly. I wanted to ask him about my brother as he was getting into a lot of trouble with the wrong sort of people. So, I asked Nicky, "Do you want to try?" and he agreed even though I could see he did not believe.

I did everything as I had seen the girls do in school. I arranged the letters of the alphabet in a circle with yes and no at either end. I said a prayer into a cup to bless us on our journey and placed it into the center of the circle, upon which we placed our fingers. I asked two or three times, "Troy can you hear us if so, move the glass to yes." The glass began to move slowly towards yes. My brother looked on in utter disbelief at his own eyes and said I was trying to trick him. I told my brother to ask him anything personal that only he and Troy would know. What he asked alludes me, but what I do know is, after the answer he received, tears fill in his eyes and I could sense he was now a believer.

I asked Troy about Nicky and he clearly spelt out that if he continued the life he was living, then he would end up the same way as him. He also said not to tell my gran about talking to him, as it would upset her too much, a silence I have held for many decades. He also said he loved his dad, my granddad who he did not particularly get on with

21

in life.

Without warning my mind started to tell me that my body was getting tired, so I asked Troy, "Are you tired, do you want to sleep?" which he replied, "Yes." Nicky, who was now very much engrossed in the experience did not want Troy to leave, but reluctantly he said goodbye. I could see the pain in his eyes however, the experience never ended there.

Nicky somehow had summoned an ex-girlfriend maybe through the power of his thought, who had died in a car accident at a young age. He wanted to know why she finished with him. She relayed her parents would not have approved of her seeing a black boy. He laughed as if he already knew. At that point, my mind started to tell my body that I was feeling tired and drained and that I needed to rest. I told Nicky that we had to stop as I felt I could not go on anymore. I felt an over whelming sense of pressure surrounding my whole being even though I could feel no pain. Reluctantly he agreed to end the session and the experience was over, or so I thought.

I could not shake the feeling that I had been put on this path for a reason and that it was far from coincidence or misfortune that I experienced the things I did. In its entirety, I laid this responsibility at the foot of my mother's door. Locked in spiritual warfare with all her notions, potions and special bathes, it was mother who had initiated me into the realms of whatever, when I was about twelve years old. As I flick through my album of memories my sister and I are crouched naked in a bath and there is a black woman with no face who holds a knife in one hand and a pigeon in the other that does not coo neither flutter in fear.

With a swipe of her knife, I feel the warm blood of pigeon trickle down my back. Just like in a silent movie depicting sound through expression, I see Cecile jump out of the bath throwing her arms around wildly as if fighting off the un-seen. Whatever was being done, she didn't like it or wanted it, so the blood only touched her partially.

Through this mayhem still crouched in my naked position, I remained perfectly calm and still. Even though I had never experienced anything like that before it did not perturb or disturb me because I knew what ever mum brought forth to me, only came with love and so I trusted in her judgement one hundred percent.

Looking back, it pains me to remember for I know with all of mother's best intentions to protect her young, it was still wrong. The forces she had summoned to do good works came from an unclean source. Mother's misgivings had laid invitations for the spirits of anarchy to run amuck with her family and for some reason, I had been chosen to fight that battle. I had found a strange comfort in having some understanding as to the possible whys and how's of my complex life which made a lot more sense than, "Shit happens." Never the less, it still did not prepare me for the spiritual journey I was about to take that would test my mental and physical fortitude to its limits.

It would appear from the moment I made contact with my uncle, the initiation that took place a year ago had finally been completed a year later and by my own doing. As if drawn by instinct, like bees to honey, I had created an umbilical cord that linked my reality to that of the spirits in the sky. The strangest of things started happening to me. I started to have vivid and disturbing dreams, the kind of dreams that feel real, dreams that I instinctively understood but could not explain.

Like Pandora's box, I had opened something I had no understanding of or the powers that governed it and it frightened the life out of me. Unconsciously I had exposed myself to the mysteries and miracles of the unexplainable and this one night which was to be a major turning point in my life spiritually, I knew for sure there were other forces at work that where not of this world yet existed within it.

I had returned home late one evening with a can of orange tango in my hand. I went straight up to my room which was at the front of the house with double windows. I closed my bedroom curtains as I did every night and put the can down on my dresser which was in alignment with the window on the left side. On the left side of the dresser was my bed which was separated by a chair in between. I sat on my bed and at some point, fell asleep. I'm not quite sure how long for, but when I awoke the curtains on the left-hand side of the room had been drawn open. Mother was down stairs in the kitchen pottering about and Nicky was in his bedroom getting ready to go out.

When I peered into the window, I could see the reflection of my room however, it was all in technicolor and resembled a cartoon type of visual. However, something bothered me about this visual. There was something in the reflection from the window that I could not see in my room. In the chair positioned at the head of my bed sat a man with a crown on his head. I rubbed my eyes in disbelief and looked again. The image never moved.

Not sure if I had smoked to much ash the night, I decided to call my brother in and get his take on things. Remaining quite calm at this point, I sat him down on the bed beside me and said, "Do you see anything in the window?" and he replied, "No." So, I thought, idea! Knowing a bit about physics, I asked, "Can you see the reflection of the can in the window?" I kept re-affirming with him, "If it is dark on the outside and light on the inside, you get a reflection, everyone knows that, right?" As he leaned forward squinting his eyes to see what he clearly could not, he admitted he couldn't see the cans reflection even though I was holding it in my hand waving it up and down franticly.

Not only was there no reflection of the can, there was no reflection of us. I began to shit myself as a feverish panic came over me. I was sure what I was seeing, that no one else could see was going to turn ugly. As my mind raced over all the scenes from the Hammer House of Horrors and the Tales of The Unexpected, I let out an almighty scream that must have awoke the dead.

Mum came rushing upstairs from the kitchen saying, "What's the matter? What's the matter?" She looked more flustered by the noise I was making as opposed to the reason why I was acting hysterical. "There's something in the window," I screeched as I buried my head deep into my brother's chest. "There's nothing there, there's nothing there," she kept saying, as she closed back the curtains. With that she turned away and went back downstairs to the kitchen.

Not truly convinced by her calmness or absentness to comfort me when she could see I was more than just upset, I ran to her bedroom and jumped into her bed. I thought I would be safe there. Trembling with fear, curled into the tiniest ball I could make, I clutched the bible and repeated, "The Lord is my shepherd I shall not want."

Now, mother liked having big glass bottles filled with water laying around the house. There was one such bottle placed in the corner by the entrance of her bedroom door which stood beside a white marble effect wardrobe, which over looked the bed and was in perfect alignment of the bedroom window. As sure as I was born black, I saw a figure of a man in a black cape and a Zorro type hat immerge out of the bottle heading straight towards me.

Barley coming to terms with what I had just seen not ten minutes ago my body began to vibrate, my heart had enthused itself to my mouth, as my lower jaw began an immediate descent. Tilting my head slightly to the left and then to the right with eyes sprawled wide, firmly poised in indecisiveness at what I was seeing that nobody else could see I let out an almighty, "Ah, there's something coming out of the water."

As if on cue to my screams Nicky comes running into mum's room naked as a baby, "What's wrong? What's wrong?" he says, by which time mum comes rushing up the stairs. "Get back into your room and put some clothes on," she shouts. "There's something coming out of the water," I shouted emphatically. She pauses for a moment at the sight of my hysteria and thought not to embrace me or calm me down even though I clutched the bible like a forgotten child raised by wolves. Instead she gave me that look, that look I had once given her in her moment of hysteria and too did nothing. She turned her back on me and went downstairs. I could hear pots and pans clinking, water running, I knew she was making something, more potions, I guess. Nicky decided to stay in that night, he said, "It must be a sign not to go out."

Alone in my mind, lost in total incomprehension at what I was experiencing I lay tucked in my perfect ball as I watched on how this thing immerged from the bottle, aligned itself in the dead center of the wardrobe revealing its true shadow form letting me know, whilst I was clearly looking at it, it was clearly looking at me.

Materializing from water into a full shadow of a man whose figure stood like an odium of darkness, dominate in its stance and nature, it swallowed up nearly every space of white of the wardrobe to be seen. I couldn't take my eyes off it. I felt as if a plague had been released upon me and my fate had been sealed to the shadows for tampering with the un-known. It had revealed its presence to be real, as real as I am alive therefore making it something I could not ignore.

Mum finally came up stairs with some garlic tea, which she insisted that I drink. She stayed in the bedroom with me thereon after and did not venture back downstairs. As she turned off the bedroom light and got into bed, the light from the moon shone brightly through the window onto the wardrobe illuminating the area like a stage yet, the shadow did not flinch neither fade. Mum didn't have any curtains up at the time. It seemed as if the moon was the spotlight for it to shine. I asked mum, "What's that figure on the wardrobe?" With no expression she replied, "Oh, it must be from something in the room." I looked at her in utter amazement for my intelligence knew there was nothing in that room that could make a perfect shadow of a man. Her excuses told me she too could see it, maybe she even saw what was in my bedroom window, so I simply replied, "There is no object in this room that could make that shape." We exchanged no more words after that for the rest of the night.

To alert to sleep I kept saying the Lord's Prayer until the figure eventually disappeared in timing of the sun arising. That was the first and last time I saw the shadow in its form, but its presence remained like decaying residue taunting me, watching me from my bedroom window. I knew it couldn't hurt me, but it didn't stop me from feeling freaked out. Its presence was foreboding and always seemed strongest when there was a crisis in the house. A rotating web of chaos had been sprung with trip wires everywhere ready to feed on vulnerability at the smallest of triggers.

This nonphysical being that dispersed seeds of doom into the atmosphere, that was as real as the air I know I breathed, wanted self-destruction and certain annihilation of me and my family. I wondered could this be the face of madness that mum saw at her point of her turning. Like me she also had dreams, gave warnings of things to come and saw things that no one else could see. Could it be that indeed mum was not mad, but actually seeing the world as it really was and that we, "Normal people," were the ones who had lost sanity a long time ago, living obliviously to the forces that surround and manipulate us?

It's enough to drive anyone mad truly, such is the power of knowledge. I wondered what fate awaited my mind? For if I too like mother were having visions, giving warnings, dreaming of things yet to come but no myself to be sane, then am I not in fact mad too.

This propels me to a dream I had many moons forward, which makes sense as to what was happening back then. The devil felt sure that I was going to join him, Why? I don't know. What pack could I have possibly made that he felt so assured in me? He was beaming with triumph at the deal he had struck, if it is possible for him to feel such a thing. Through his imageless face I could see his definition that was sharp at every angle. His eyes where blacker than any black I had ever seen. Standing six feet tall and then some, cast in black iron, he oozed confidence.

When he realized that I was a sworn defender of good and that I rebuked the devil with his fiery breath of pestilence and un-forgiveness, he proclaimed, "I'm going to get you for that." I knew this included anyone that I loved. He was determined to shatter the very heart of me slowly and then the battle began. Upon the battle field eight demons and angels appeared. One by one, they disappeared until there was two. I was told to flee, that I had to survive. It was then I knew the journey I had been placed on for whatever reason was one that only I alone could take.

Without a doubt that was my reality. Alone in my mind, locked in spiritual war for the life of my future to come, I tried hard to hold onto the last grains of my family. I understood that everything was destined never to be the same again. So much of what was had been removed from my foundation, there was barely a trace to be seen. My anxieties of Nicky not being around were at its peak, he was my last safe place. The thought of losing him would yank my heartstrings viciously making me feel physical pain reducing me to floods of tears. It is then I recall mum kicking Nicky out of the home.

I don't know what triggered the argument between them, but it ended with Nicky trashing his bedroom and mummy screaming her head off, "Get out." My brother was crying, something I rarely saw him do. He looked broken and in despair with a look that said, I love you, but I can't do this no more. I could see he had had enough of the in-house madness mummy was keeping up. He wanted things back to normal as I did but it just wasn't going to happen. Immobilized by fear to stop the fight I did nothing but look on as I watched him walk out of our once loved home and out of my life leaving me to fend for myself, something I thought he would always do for me.

I never thought that, that chain would be broken, but it was and when it did, so broke my heart. I was now isolated from everyone. Who would look out for me now? Who would I talk to when things got too much for me? When he left, he took a piece of me with him and I know a piece of mum went with him too, mother's little champion, a name she gave to him herself.

I had always received mums favor for being a good girl, but it was Nicky who was her favorite. On one occasion, I remember mother having a chaotic moment, a tab I picked up regularly. Yet somehow in her incoherent moment she was coherent enough to tell me that if she had to choose between my brother and me, she would choose him. I couldn't be sure if mum was really mad in what appeared to be a conscious effort to deliberately hurt me, which she did. I felt those words like hot coals beneath my feet, it burned and then some.

It's Time to Cleanse

Day by day, piece by piece I watched all that I had grown with, all that was familiar to me, all that meant something to me placed with great precision into black bags and put outside in the rubbish for any passerby to browse and consider. It's a bit like spring-cleaning except mum was emptying the entire contents of our home. It was frustrating enough that I had literally been stripped of my future memories and a life I had been accustomed to, I now had to give up the comforts of my home, the last memory bank of my heart, I felt so dislocated.

I found myself attaching sentiment to everything in the house, down to the discarded toy part that laid abandoned for years underneath my bed. Those pieces of rubbish were more valuable to me than anything money could buy. It sounds stupid, but when I held those lost parts in my hands it created a porthole in my mind that took me back to a place when I was happy. It was the only way I knew how to keep my memories alive.

One fine morning mother began her crusade of freeing herself of stuff and decided to throw out her **100% WOOL & SILVER FOX COAT**. Now I know mother was committed to the cause of ridding herself of everything that even smelt like the past, but surely not this coat. To have something like that in the early 80s was expensive and exclusive and mother did like the best things in life. Not fully understanding the implications of animal cruelty, I regarded this coat as one of my mother's greatest price possessions. I never knew or saw anyone in anything like it and anytime mother put it on she always laughed and pranced as if in love. I would watch her with starry eyes thinking I can't wait to try on the coat when she goes out. I could never have dreamt that mother would dispose of it. The mere thought exceeded my mental capacity to comprehend the notion of, possibility.

This was a woman adored and admired by many for her clothes and style of dress. The wigs were endless, the shoes countless, the makeup and the accessories where to die for, something I took full advantage of when playing dress up. However, like everything else that had gone out in the rubbish so did the coat.

It was strange to watch mum behave completely detached from any emotions when I knew she came from a place of great love and affection. It sent a subliminal message that paralyzed my reactive system placing me as an observer to my own fate. I felt lost in a maze of disbelief, as the things that once ignited a fire in me were ousted without a second glance.

I remember looking out of my bedroom window, which over looked the street and clocked a tramp walking in the direction of, **MY HOUSE**. As thoughts of, "Rescue the coat," raced through my mind, I toyed with the possibility that this might not really be happening even though I knew my own eyes were baring witness. I didn't want to admit that it would soon be gone forever.

Over whelmed with helplessness I watched on as the tramp reached our house and noticed the **100% WOOL & SILVER FOX COAT** in the bin as they do. He pauses briefly scanning his surroundings like a true scavenger and then with caution pulls it out of the bag and examines it. I couldn't be sure if he was surprised at his find or just a fussy tramp. After several minutes of deliberation, he nods his head to himself and then walks off with it. He must have been thinking that's beer money for tonight.

Disabled by my age that once gave me power to dictate change, I knew once that **100% WOOL & SILVER FOX COAT** was gone it would be like losing Tabby, my step dad, my sister, my brother, mum and my childhood all over again. I must have stood in the same spot for some ten minutes after the tramp had gone, just looking at the empty black bag that was once filled with my memories. I couldn't help but think, "Why had any old passerby been allowed to pick up a piece of me and go about his business unchallenged?" I was incapable to do anything about it, just like everything else that had departed from my life. I was so angry with hurt that day, I wanted to cry so much but the tears just would not flow.

Whatever mother was trying to purge herself of she was determined to leave no stone unturned and continued religiously to touch every room, every corner and every crevice of the house. She'd often decode the house of its homely elements removing familiarity and replacing it with oddity. There were slashes of different paints on the wall in random places, or dirt piled in the corners with bits of this and that and dead flowers. The cooker was now a work surface, we no-longer flushed the toilet we poured water down it and the bath and wash basin became another storage space for, things. I now washed in the bucket.

You could see in the midst of disorder that everything was strategically cleaned, removed and placed, enhancing the no atmospheric warmth. Even the natural light that came through the windows seemed suppressed around the edges. The more things disappeared or became defaced by mum, the more I became aware of a constant gloom that lay like fog in the house where happy feelings could not thrive or survive, it was eerie. Like Jacob's ladder my life images where being distorted by my mind's eye and nothing seemed to be what it really was in the here and now.

I came from a large family network that always said they loved me, so why did I feel so alone? Why? Why? Why? Why bloody me? I carried questions in my veins with no tangible answers to be found. In my head, I wanted to do the right thing, be strong and soldier through like a trooper, yet all I felt I was doing was standing still. I was caught in a dazed cycle whilst the world passed me over. Why had they abandoned me so?

I hated being the only one in the world who cared because it meant sacrificing my life like a lamb to the slaughter and I didn't even know who I was yet. I was just a kid and I expected my peers who knew best and whom I'd looked up to for most of my life to see beyond my fake smile or brave face and intervene. But it never did quite happen that way.

All alone with no one to give me direction and protect me from myself, I chose to live a life I thought my mum would have liked me to lead. There was still a part of me that was heavily under the influence that if I did well and not get into any trouble, I would get a reward. The prize being getting my mum back the way I used to remember her and having the house back in order looking tip top with the sounds of my folks chattering away in broken French and my brother and sister talking or arguing as the case may be.

I couldn't have wanted for anything different because I didn't know any different, so I openly wished that what mum was going through was just a passing phase. The truth is mum had, had spouts of behaving oddly in the past. For some reason the times, occasions and events never really stuck in my mind. I just knew they had happened before, but it was never as bad as this. I can't remember seeing her sobbing her heart out over a man or neglecting to do her hair.

Mummy was a qualified manicurist and masseur, she knew about taking care of herself inside and out. Always meticulous about her weight she took pride in her battle against the bulge. More importantly, I was proud of her. I was proud that she had raised three children on her own and had a nice home with things that most people envied. I felt truly blessed that I was my mother's daughter. Nothing was more important than the love of mummy. The thing was, I was living on past memories of my mother's love and no longer knew if she loved me in the here and now.

At home time did not exist as I once knew it. Home had become a porthole to hell. Everything seemed to happen that little bit slower, a turning of the head, a blink of an eye, or a slap in the face. Time at home gave me an awareness of the different dimensions in which I lived. It had begun to consume me.

One morning I was pretending to confer with my imaginary friends as you do about everything and nothing. When suddenly, I stopped my gibbering mid-flow to listen to the faint chattering in the background. It was mother talking to herself about everything and nothing too. I shouted down to her, "Didn't you think that this would rub off on me?" she did not reply. Not only did I talk to myself a lot more, I would imagine myself in situations that were full of misery, loss, death and abandonment. I remember crying on many occasions to my fake stories displaying the heart wrenching emotions as if they were real.

I was confused and mentally exasperated not only by mother but by the house with all its bricks and mortar. It somehow seemed to drain my energy every time I entered it. I swear blind that it was alive and breathed uncertainty into the atmosphere, thriving off the chaos that ran rampant. I became afraid of my once loved home just like my mother and never entered it when I knew I would be alone. Home had become the bloody battlefield upon which I had to lay my head, subjected to the nightly cries of torture. Desperately wanting to close my eyes but too afraid to dream, I'd imagine myself away and survive the nightly calamity.

I wore many masks to masquerade the inner me, so the real world wouldn't see that I was different. It didn't require much effort because people are so caught up in their problems. In the mass of walking afflicted I was a mere dot on the map, hard to notice and easily forgotten. I carried the legacy of Zorro, master of disguise, elusive in my tracks, friends of many but known by few. No one knows the aches and pains of his weary heart and anyone who did were either dead, murdered or soon to be. Trusting no one or placing his life in the hands of any one man is his key to staying alive. As fictional as it sounds, that felt like me, hiding behind a mask to protect my identity. Pretending to be someone that I wasn't was easy enough and even fun at times however, like all things in life, everything has its sell by date.

Out there somewhere in the elements of space, my sense of belonging and normality were slowly trickling away from me, frequently leaving me questioning my own sanity. If I do some of the things that mummy does and I can understand what she saying even when I know she's speaking a dialect and language that does not exist, does that mean that I too am like mummy? Wherever I heard the word, "Normal," it triggered signals to my brain that said, "What am I?"

I felt like an outcast by circumstance and a jailer of my own thoughts. I was living a double life, double jeopardy more likes. Everyone I knew had a mother who showed him or her love and cooked them meals at night. I just wanted to be able to sit down, talk, and laugh with mines as we used to. Maybe even return to a warm inviting home now and then, instead of having to re-invent myself based on ideals that had long since passed.

Unlike the films, reality has its ugly way of setting in like rigor mortis and doesn't end with the main characters making it through their troubled times. I was slipping into a depression of my own whilst mum's condition progressively got worse. She seemed to be besieged by the need to be transformed into anything different than who she was. She was trying to reinvent her life that was slowly erasing mine. Choice was never in the equation once madness moved in. I had been set upon a path that had no logical answers or questions, it was just so. All I could do was ride the waves best I could and pray for a better tomorrow.

Once again change was on the move shifting the goal posts of time. I now faced a reconditioning of displacement once removed finalizing the demolition of, the good old days. Not only had my surroundings been altered beyond remembering, my vocabulary was now to follow suite. I was to encompass a new way of behaving that was nothing like being Shavon. Mum had developed a new personality along her journey of lost and found, that rebuked the word, mother, and detested offspring. She was angry and didn't give a dam who knew it. One fine day that personality took a name and that name was, Pauline, and that was how I was to refer to her, my mum, for the next couple years of my life.

Pauline

Now Pauline could be a nasty bit of work when she was ready, she had no maternal feelings and resented the fact that she had to take care of me. I was the burden she could have done without and therefore became the focus of all her anger. My first introduction to Pauline was when I was having a seemingly normal day with mum. Our personal belongings were not being put in the trash and the destruction of the house had ceased.

Mum and I had been out the day to see if she could sell her car, a blue beetle she had, had sat outside the house for some time. Everything seemed calm and normal. So calm and normal it reminded me of, "The good old days." So, convinced was I that things had resumed itself in my mother's head and that we were back on track to the, "Normal road," I allowed myself to get drunk in the wondrous feeling of, "Finally, she's back."

I started to view the day in a completely new light. It was almost blinding beyond belief, I could not hold back the massive grin that over took my face. The taste of happiness had me craving for more like a pregnant woman for food. I was eager to slip back into my role of let's pretend so I started to joke around trying to prompt mum to laugh. I wanted her to feel as I did, full of beans and delighted with the new revelations that, things were back to normal.

However, like Dr. Jackal and Mr. Hyde, mother switched on me. Civility had been thrown out the window and I was confronted with an expressionless steer and words of, "You're a filthy little whore, you're a slut, you fail, you fe dead. And don't call me mummy, call me Pauline." Just like that. I swear blind the whole street heard my mum curse me that day.

The veins in her neck were jutting out stiff like cardboard and her eyes were filled with such rage that I could no longer see the whites, everything looked black. I kept wondering if she could really see me. Completely knocked for six at the density and magnitude of force used to insult me, I seemed to respond as if on cue to a stage show I had written. My little face began an immediate withdrawal as my body posture made its descent south, finding its resting place between nothingness and numbness. Realizing that I had miscalculated the situation getting it terribly wrong, I had opened the floodgates for aftermath which left me feeling afraid. It was a year later that I remember smiling again after that incident.

Pauline became more insulting within that year of meeting her. I could always tell when she was present. Her body language became void of any emotion and a stern facial expression would appear. Like a lucid dream her behavior grew vile and disturbing as she developed bad habits like spitting buckets of saliva and flem onto the house walls as she cursed her profanities. "Why don't you lick shit, you filthy little whore, you dirty little cunt. You fail, you fail." She would often say that to me.

Pauline did not worry or care for my feelings. Her intent was to hurt me for when she looked at me, she saw something horrible and nasty. I, according to Pauline was meant to be dead. That could not be true enough. My sister told me a story when I was about eleven years old that mum tried to throw herself down the stairs when she knew she was pregnant with me.

My sister only told me that story to knock down the pedestal I had placed mum upon, but it served a greater purpose, it filled me with compassion. For a moment in time, I visualized my mother standing at the top of the stairs, heavily pregnant, dressed in her brown nightgown. Her hair is unkempt, and she looks distressed as she closes her eyes in desperation and just falls.

I felt empathy for her. I embraced the turmoil and agony she must have went through as if it were I and wanted to be at the foot of the stairs to catch her fall. I could not find it in myself to be angry with my mother for the things she had done in her past, for I had seen the hard work she had done in her present. I loved her and behind all the spheres of hurt thrown at me, I believed that if she were in her right frame of mind, she would not be doing some of the things she had. It was a hard pill to swallow but I did it all the same.

Mechanically, I settled into my new routine of doings things at home. I would get up at around 7.00am. Pauline would greet me at the foot of my bedroom door with an almighty wallop around the face then walk off as if nothing had happened. I too would follow suite and show no

41

emotion or reaction. I would then go downstairs into the kitchen, get the hand broom and sweep the stairs from top to bottom. After that I'd get myself washed, dressed and leave for school.

I'm not sure when the routine stopped but it appeared to last forever. I tried my best to understand my complex and unexplainable predicament, but the harder I'd tried the more disappointed and disillusioned I became. I tried for a while at being the good little girl that kept her mouth shut. I tried to be the soft place to fall. I tried to keep it all together by myself. I tried, I tried, and I tried some more.

I soaked up all the negative energy like a sponge, unaware that at some unpredictable moment all that energy would need to seep its way out. I could not have foreseen it seeping like a raging torrent with its uncontrollable need to break free from man-made boundaries that restrain and prohibit its line of flow. On my ever-decreasing circle to nowhere, I was lending a hand in destroying my only hope weighted down by my own hearts psyche. It was becoming challenging to see the woods through the trees.

One morning I awoke feeling broken and in bits. I had tried many ways to let people know that my spirit was dyeing and that I needed help. Yet on deaf ears my cries had fallen, whilst seeing eyes looked me over. I awoke wanting the world to know I was crying. I wanted my family to feel my pain and most of all I wanted my mum to get some help. Firmly anchored to my chain of madness, exasperated by my routine lie of being miss happy go lucky shit, I decided that enough was enough and that it was time for radical action. There was nothing left but to offer the ultimate sacrifice, a solution no one else could offer, my life.

How I thought removing myself would make it better I don't know, but at the time it seemed to make sense. Mother no longer loved me, which she habitually reinforced. I understood that I was the source of all her disappointments that clearly added to her problems instead of alleviating them. No one seemed to care enough of how eaten up inside I was which further enhanced that dead to life feeling. I didn't want to be a part of a world that scattered its careless opinions around like loose change, thriving on superficial love that's only prepared to stand up and be counted behind closed doors. I was a problem that no one wanted to deal with which in my mind justified what I was about to do.

Meticulously I had planned my exit for a Friday after I had finished a week at school, giving me enough time to savior memories of laughter with all my friends who were unaware of my plans to suddenly depart. In my mind's eye, there was no going back no matter what. All I wanted to do was create a sense of joy that would last for just a little while. I resented the fact I had become accustomed to being non-applicable.

When I returned home that afternoon, I searched the house high and low for any form of medication. In mid flow, I remembered that mother had exterminated the house of everything and anything that had purpose. All I could find was a bottle of vitamin E pills and a razor blade that was miraculously left in the kitchen draw. "Must be my lucky day," I said allowed.

As I walked up the stairs from the kitchen to my bedroom, with no time to waste I furiously hacked away at my left wrist. As I clinched my teeth with my eyes tightly shut, I dug deep as though digging for treasure. I desperately wanted to see the gushing of blood, so the journey of release could begin, but the blasted thing wouldn't cut. It just left big indentations on my wrist. I had to study the razor blade hard to be sure my eyes weren't deceiving me. So, I tested it on my thumb, oh it was real and sharp enough to cut, but for some reason, it wouldn't slash my wrists. Perplexed and filled with tears, I cast the blade aside and thought it will have to be plan b, take as many pills as possible.

Time being of the essence I hurried to wash and prepare myself for bed. I put on my nicest nightgown and lit the half burnt out candle on my dresser to see me through the night. I asked God, "Forgive me for the sin I am about to commit and try and understand that what I am doing, I am doing for the greater good of mum. Forgive me. Amen." This was my last ditched attempt to make the impossible right and even though the light at the end of the tunnel resembled eternal death, it was a small sacrifice to make for a worthy cause by far.

Crouching low by the stairs on the landing outside my bedroom, I spied through the spindles with squinted eyes for signs of mother's silhouette venturing upstairs. With one ear half coxed, I proceeded to take as much pills as my tiny little stomach could hold. At one point a vile oily after taste sized the back of my throat. It was the vitamin E, it tasted like excrement that almost caused me to vomit. But so, determined was I to fulfill my mission, I took the fleeting recess as an opportunity to refocus my mind on why I was doing this. With a nod of my head and rapid blinking of the eyes, I convinced myself it was the right thing to do and continued the task at hand.

As soon as I had swallowed the last pill in the bottle my mind seemed to rid itself of any emotion. My whole being went into lifeless mode. A bit like when you see those Egyptians movies where the queen appears to accept her fate to be sealed in a tomb alive. There was no regret or remorse in my heart, there was just validation, the ends justifying the means and all that. All I could see before me was phase two which was to lay in bed, close my eyes and allow sleep to take me away at its will.

There was no more time to deliberate on the rights or wrongs of life. There were no more chances to make it right for the door that led to talk was now closed. The deed had been done as swift as the seed was planted in my head. All what was left, was for nature to take its course and end what I had started.

To me, I thought this would conclude all the confusion that seemed to dominate my mother's life. Finally, I would do something right for mum, even though I gave no thought as to what might happen to her state of mind finding me dead in my bed. I really was not able to think that far ahead, I just wanted the hurt to go away. As I closed my eyes with peace in my heart, I let my mind wonder to where ever it wanted to go. I was surrendering myself to the power of the vitamin E with the hope it would do as I requested and rid mum of me, the last remaining reminder of all her suffering to which she seemed eternally bound. I closed my eyes.

I am not sure when day broke, I just knew I had to arise. I awoke in the same position as I had gone to sleep, lying on my back, arms crossed over my chest and toes erected. I took my time and opened my eyes. As I looked about my surroundings, I knew I was still in my bed, yet repeatedly I asked myself, "Am I in heaven or stuck in my room for eternity for taking my own life?" I was nervous at the thought of, where am I? yet my body remained calm and perfectly still.

As the night's sleep started to wear off and the, "I'm still alive!" senses started to kick in, I realized I had failed in my quest. How could this be? Why was I still here? Not only could I not slit my own wrists, I couldn't even complete a successful over dose. Utterly demoralized I spent the whole Saturday feeling useless and a failure. What could I possibly do for my situation when I could not even get killing myself right? What hope was there for me?

I decided to go for a walk down the local park hoping with space my mind could breathe. On my journey, I saw my sister walking about her business. "Cecile," I yelled as I automatically burst into floods of tears. She embraced me and said, "What's wrong?" I couldn't tell her of what I had just done but surely, she knew there were problems at home. Why else would I be crying inconsolably in the middle of the street? The words, "Its mummy," could not transcend from my mouth. I somehow figured she already knew what I wanted to say but too afraid to ask, she continued, "Is everything all right at home? What's wrong?" Taking this, as a sign of avoidance I replied, "Nothing, I'll be alright." I bravely wiped away my tears, pulled myself together, and with a final, "I'm alright man, I'm alright," I pulled back, said goodbye and continued my journey to the park alone.

As I walked away in slumber, I thought is it a wonder I feel alone. How broken did I have to look before somebody, anybody would intervene, take control? What did I have to do to get their attention? Overcome by my new-found friend called numbness, I found myself drifting in the park to end up sitting on some bench somewhere.

As I sat for some ten minutes searching through the sky trying to see beyond the clouds for a sign of hope, which I never saw, I caught myself gently rocking to and froe. A thought of, "Oh my God, I'm sitting on a park bench rocking, if I let go, who's going to catch me when I fall? I need to get my shit together." As soon as I posed the question to myself, I stopped rocking and just kept looking at the sky as if I was waiting for a miracle.

If anyone was watching me, they must have thought, this girl's mad. They wouldn't have been far off. Firstly, I failed in my botched attempt to take my own life due to inadequate equipment and secondly, I'm now sat rocking on a park bench looking up at the sky as if I've seen someone I know. Just like love and hate so too is a thin line between sane and insane and for some reason it had placed itself before my feet.

Insane was tempting me with, "If you want to let go, then let go. Why should you have to bear the brunt of everything? Let someone else take the slack. Why don't you come over to my place? Just let go of your mind and slip right in?" Sane on the other hand was saying, "Now you've seen the heartache and turmoil of living in the madness, is that what you want to become? Besides, who is going to be there for you if you fall. Find another way."

Clearly, I was having major battles in my tiny brain. Letting go seemed to have so much appeal even for just a moment but ultimately, I knew it was a transparent web of chaos to have me up just like my mum. Sane had won the battle this time, but I knew it wouldn't be long before war would be wagered against me tempting me once again to cross the line.

As I intravenously force fed myself happy thoughts trying hard to pacify the anarchy that was running amuck in my mind, I decided I needed a booster to suppress the remaining surplus of crap that happy thoughts just would not fix. I found myself walking the path to the off license and then to the herbs man. I remember my legs feeling so weak that day I could just about carry my seven and a half stone body to the shops. I knew something was going to give sooner or later and I knew it would be me to suffer the consequences, but I felt powerless to stop it from happening. Whether I liked it or not my system of survival was shutting itself down and my memory storage space was no longer receiving data.

Filled to the nostrils with bits of this and pieces of that, every breath I took felt like a struggle because it meant more time to feel and more time to feel meant more pain. I tried hard to stop my mind spilling over like a penny jar crashing hard to the ground with its particles scattering far and wide to places you'd thought it couldn't possibly reach. But unable to control what was happening around me or to me, I subconsciously placed my life into the hands of, "Who gives a shit," and began a self-cleansing of my own called, "Fuck it."

Manifestation

Little by little, I started to over indulge in drink and smoking puff, acquiring the nickname, "Mash Up." It was very rare for me to be non-intoxicated. I was of the mind-set that everything's worth trying at least once. Alcohol or drugs it made no difference to me. Unlike my friends I wasn't experimenting for a laugh. For me getting high and being out of it was the one tool that supplied me with the escapism from my world. It hurt that I couldn't face it yet eased me somewhat when things got too much. However, through trial and error I found that the after effects of certain particularly drugs just weren't for me. They seem to amplify the feelings of not being in control of my own senses that made the presence of loneliness too apparent, only serving to further highlight my vulnerabilities in its chipped away state.

School bore the brunt for most of my rebelliousness. Don't get me wrong I loved school, it was the one place I truly felt at ease. It was the perfect breeding ground for child-like behavior. It was easier to disguise drunken and disorderly behavior on the lack of awareness of the influence of alcohol and drugs due to my immaturity and inexperience of life. The reality behind that mask was, I could be irresponsible, reckless and blame it all on something else, just like a normal teenager, if only but for a while.

It frustrated me that I had to create distractions from certain topics as simple as, what you watched the night before because mother put the TV out in the rubbish. It sounds minor, but I so wanted the latest coat in fashion, so I could say my mum bought it for me. I always seemed to have variations of what was in, but not quite the same. How we take for granted the things we think will never end. If only I had known that innocent moments shared would be gone forever, I would have cherished them more.

The saddest moment about school was home time. When the last pips went, you'd hear a herd of trampling feet some running, shuffling, some skipping. The sound of, ramping filled the ear ways and the corridors. I too would follow suite and join the rush in pursuit of the school gates to link my friends for the journey home. Most of my friends lived in the same area so I was effortlessly enthused with laughter and jokes on the buses coming home. We'd sing songs, tell jokes, pretend to speak in a different language, trace each other and occasional get someone to miss their bus stop. I loved it until that is, when it was my turn to get off.

I'd maintain my happy face waving extra fast until the bus drove away. As soon as it did my eyes would revert to the floor, as I'd begin my aimless shuffle home perplexed by my own inner voice, "Your nearly home. Won't be long now, back to whatever." I constantly felt reminded of where

I didn't want to be. So, every time I said that last, "See you later," I did so with passion for I truly could not predict what tomorrow would bring.

When I used to visit my best friend's house, my heart would always feel heavy as I soaked up the atmosphere of family dynamics, the smell of cooking and the chastisement of mum saying, "Turn down that music." Where there were good times to be had, I made sure I made the most of it for I knew in advance how temporary good times could be. Apart of me wanted to be them, for through them, I could visualize what my own family would be like if things were different. I liked remembering however, it always ended with, "But it's not like that anymore." Some days I could cope with it, but most days I blocked. There was no real time for healing or recovery, I was a walking open wound, susceptible to pick up unwanted infections.

Often, I would purposely cross the road blindly and pray a car would knock me over where upon a small crowd would shadow my lifeless body and watch me take my last breath. Likewise, late at night and feeling high, I would find myself wandering the streets, frequenting the parks, taking the longest route home. There is an old Jamaican saying, "Walk long way draw sweat. Walk short cut draw blood." I wanted to draw blood. Often men who knew better would say to me "You shouldn't be out this time of night little girl." Disillusioned by my peer's reluctance to do more and feeling totally destitute by my mother, I was convinced that I would only get to the light at the end of the tunnel if I were battered and disheveled or even better still dead. It's funny how the most illogical way of comprehending a situation can seem so logical to the person walking those footsteps.

I thought if I could show that I was physically hurt then the setting would be right, the cast would fall into action and then the gateway would open to reveal my true internal torment. Often, I'd cry floods of tears for imaginary horrific disasters where death was forever present and display signs of physical woe as if it were real. I would imagine lying in hospital looking seriously battered and bruised ranting and raving, crying my heart out because some bastard hurt me and left me for dead. My family would be sitting at my bedside watching me with remorseful eyes for what they wished they should have done but never did, as the doctors sedate me to prevent me from propelling out of control.

I found it easier to let out my emotions for something that hadn't happen because I knew once I stopped imagining, so too would the tears and I could be free of the pain, something I could not do in my real life. Time and again I'd question myself after the event and say, "But this isn't real Shavs, why are you crying like this?" Yet somehow for a short while I'd feel relieved as if a real burden had been lifted from my shoulders. I desperately wanted to be normal but a part of me felt what I was doing was mad and worse still I couldn't help it. It was a comfort to have a place to escape to for I had nowhere else to go.

Day-by-day I'd found myself imaging my mind away, spiraling to the depths of darkness just like mother Pauline. The situation wasn't eased either by her bazaar irregular behaviors. She never seemed to sleep during the night. Mother was always up in the late hours talking to herself. Even when I thought I was in the deepest of sleep I could hear her Chinese whisper in the distance. It sounded like the screeching of nails on a black board that had somehow implanted itself into the corner of my right eye and lower jaw. It irritated me big time. Then there was the obsession of burning charcoal that engulfed your air space and ran rancid in your clothes, consuming the very fabric of your skin. Most of the time I felt like I couldn't breathe.

And then there was the continuous running of water into the metal sink. It drove me insane. It was as if trapped air were in the radiators. No matter where you were in the house, you could always hear it gurgling away. It had its own unique sound that had bass on it. I used to wonder why she doesn't just turn the dam thing off. What is it with the water? Could it be a cleansing of the soul issue? Or could it be that mummy was just mad? Like all medical conditions, it seemed that things had to get worse before it got better.

For the very first time I decided to run away. I was sitting in my bedroom reminiscing over the days when I used to laugh and play with my brother and sister. I was thinking of an old Polaroid advert in the mid-70s where a girl goes into her mother's bedroom, sits at her dressing table and puts on her make up. Cute, but she looked like a clown. Anyway, the girl looks up and notices her mother watching her from the corner of the room. The girl smiles at her mother and then the mother smiles back.

Well one day Nicky decided to do just that not realizing, that things in real life within a black family are not the same as it is on television. We're all sitting in the sitting room when Nicky suddenly disappears. About five minutes later he runs back in with a big smile on his face covered in mum's makeup. She was not smiling back. "Get out of here and go and take it off," that's black people folks. He got off quite lightly considering we used to get beaten for breaking a glass. I personally thought it was sure to be a licking offence. Cecile and I started to laugh. As quick as Nicky had ran into the sitting room was as quick as he ran out. I even glimpsed a little smirk on my mother's face too. How I missed those times.

As I cracked a smiled to myself at my thoughts, I briefly forgot of my intentions to run away when suddenly, Pauline comes rushing into my room hurling abuse at me disrupting my comfort. This was all getting to be a bit too bloody much. The day before, I had had to put up with her abuse on big Stoke Newington High Street, across the road from a bus stop that happens to be the link up spot for the local residence. I had stepped above my station and decided to tell my mum what I thought of her mental state. I told her I think she is going mad. The slap she gave me in my face for my insubordination was so forceful, that I completed a full twist then a half twist out to be positioned facing my audience which just happened to be the entire neighborhood.

Now, everybody knew what I was trying so hard to hide. I did not flicker neither flinch. I held my composure, turned my head back in the direction I was meant to be walking and waited for mum's signal to move. But that wasn't enough for Pauline, to show her dominance and control, a reminder of where my place was, she decorated the final touches to her ensemble with the old verbal abuse at the top of her lungs. As at home when she finished, we continued our journey down the high street as though nothing had ever happened. Now, again today, I had to face more abuse, not a day's grace I had been given, enough was enough.

Without realizing that my legs where in motion, I found my mind running out of my bedroom, down the stair and out the front door slamming it firmly shut behind me. I didn't know where I was going but I knew I just had to go. I kept running until I found myself at the pavilion in Spring Field Park. I used to play there with my brother and sister when I was little. I bought ten B&H and proceeded to smoke them all one by one. All I kept thinking was, why is my life so fucked up? No one seems to care and if anybody does, they aren't doing anything about it. Why am I left to pick up the pieces yet I'm only a child?

I knew at some point that I would have to go home. I thought I could do what my brother did when he ran away. I could go and sleep on the floor of a taxicab for the night. However, it was early winter and there was a definite chill in the air. The thought of freezing my butt of in some old clapped out taxicab did not really appeal to me. Besides, I was very aware of the dangers that lay on the streets.

I had a friend called Kitty who I used to hang around with a lot. Our relationship was a weird one. I knew where she lived but I never went to her house, it was the same for me. We always met up on the street. I knew she had problems at home, but we never discussed it. Kitty like me would stay out late as if she too was avoiding going home. However, one day Kitty went missing. It turned out that she lay raped, beaten, brutally stabbed and left for dead in the Park. The same park I had ran away to. By the grace of God Kitty managed to crawl her way out onto the streets where she was found by a passerby.

I remember feeling sorry for her but I was so caught up in my own problems I didn't let her know that I was sorry and so I said nothing. Kitty and I never spoke again, the friendship was dissolved. The word out on the street was that she had turned to drink. Some months later in the early part of the afternoon, I saw Kitty for the first time since the incident walking down Lower Clapton road, singing loudly with her sister. As they twisted and twirled up their bodies, pissed as assholes I caught her eye briefly looking at me. I got the feeling that she wanted to say something to me but in doing so, she would have to recall her past of which I assume she was trying to forget. As I had done to her, so she had done to me and said nothing. She turned her head away and continued with her dancing and palavering. I only ever saw Kitty in passing once more years later.

He who feels it knows it. As much as I selfishly wanted to carry her pain like a chain around my neck for all to see, the reality of the mental trauma it cost her was far too overwhelming for even me to conjure up. There was no slipping into no man's land on this one. I was forced to deal with what I was going through in the here and now. I had run away from home, worst still I slammed up my mother's front door only to end up sitting all alone in a secluded part of the park where my friend was almost killed. As I puffed my lungs away never quite reaching that feeling of having had enough, my mind was searching for ways to put an end to things.

Six hours later and nine cigarettes down, I noticed the sun was starting to set and the park had emptied. I agonized with myself as to whether I should go home. I needed to make a decision before the gates were closed. Cold, damp and hungry I decided to go back home. I feared what awaited me. I came from an era where you feared your parents more than the police because your parents where the police. They were also the courts system which judged you, the prison services which carried out your correction and the media which notified the community of your status. Any disrespect can trigger that process into action and slamming up her front door and running away was such an offence.

I thought, if the life I was living felt like the end then surely for my disobedience the end was imminent. I took my time and walked home, the long route as usual. Upon my return mother had made dinner for me and had tidied the house. She acted as if nothing had happened and for the first time, it was a relief to play that game.

Like the changing of the seasons mother had taken a turn for the worst and had become nasty Pauline whom for a moment I had forgotten. It was mid-winter and the nights were bitter. One evening I came home round about nine o'clock. "Pauline", I called throw the letterbox but got no response. Mother had a habit of locking the front door from the inside and always took ages to come down the stairs to open the door. So, I decided to persevere a bit longer. As I elongated the Paul and emphasized the Lean, "Pauline," I shouted for about the 10th time. I could hear traces of movement coming from inside the house but nothing concrete and as like the first time I got no response.

At some point I remember feeling a stillness in the atmosphere. There was nothing or no one in sight. The silence rang like church bells in my ears as I thought, "Could it really be that everyone on this particular night chose to go to bed at the same time." The only movement was that of the flickering streetlights. Scared, cold, tired and unsure as to whether my mum was avoiding me, truly asleep or just in one of her zones, I decided to go around the back of the house, up the fire escape and through the back door that was un-securely boarded up with pieces of wood. I had to think long and hard about what was I prepared to do because like most things in my life at that time, even using the fire escape brought up past fears.

It was a hot summers day, I must have been about thirteen or so and I decided to sunbathe on our fire escape four flights up. As I lay on my back I decided to turn over and as I did so I nearly fell through a gap in the railings. I was not aware at the time that where I was laying there was a pole missing. In fact, within an instance of me turning over I saw the missing pole before me. It would seem as if my eyes were still closed but my brain had already been programmed to the missing pole. It was only when my hand and my shoulders felt no restraint as I turned over, that I truly opened my eyes and realized that I was about to take a very long fall. Within a split second I had secured myself and arose to my feet in disbelief as to what had just happened. I kept looking at the gap as flashes of, I know what I saw run through my mind. I started to feel uneasy and dizzy and knew I had to get off the fire escape, which I did, never to go back on it until this night.

Having weighed up the pros and cons of risking breaking my neck on the fire escape, in the dark and on a cold, breezy winters night or, sleeping on the doorstep on what seems like a very inauspicious night, I decided that I had no option. It was the fire escape or nothing.

As I digested my fears and self-respect of being some body's child, a few tears fell from my eyes onto the front of my hands. It stung from the cold as if it were burning through my skin. I quickly wiped it away on my trousers and thought, "I'll have no more of that." Dealing with my tears on top of being reduced to breaking into my own home like a thief in the night was more than I could bear.

As I reached the back door, I started to peel away the badly put together pieces of wood that replaced where the window once was. Keen not to make a whole big enough to leave the house vulnerable I made a neat little parting just big enough for me to slip through. When I entered the house all I could see was mums' rounded silhouette in shades of browns standing perfectly still at the top of stairs just looking down at me. In a calm and soft voice, she said, "Go back out the way you came." The presence in which she spoke was creepy. Mum had clearly watched me climb in even though I hadn't seen her watching me.

If madness wanted to kick off, I would have been helpless to its advances, so I never argued or tried to reason with her, I just did as I was told. I squeezed my size eight waist back through the hole, down the fire escape, through the garden, over the wall and went back to the front of the house. Half frozen and scared to death I waited ten more minutes and still mother did not come. Disheartened and saddened by the whole affair, I phoned my aunt Sybil and told her what had happened, she suggested that I come and stay by her for the night.

As soon as I arrived at my aunts' house I broke down in tears. She tried her best to comfort me, but there was nothing she could have done or said that would have made a difference to me that night. I felt misplaced and discarded like an unwanted puppy left out in the middle of the night, forced to defend itself in a world it cannot survive alone. I was angry for no matter how hard I wished tomorrow wouldn't come, I knew it would and I would have to face going home alone. The tears I cried into the pillow that night was tears of shame for not being wanted. I don't remember failing asleep, just waking up.

The next morning, as so thought, so done. I set about my journey home alone. To stubborn to ask someone to come with me and to angry that no one offered, I reserved my right to blank my thoughts until I saw mum. When I arrived home, I stood some five minutes or so looking at the front door. I was trying to see beyond the paint, wood, bricks and mortar to judge what type of reception I would get. It was no use I couldn't see a thing so, I took a deep breath, climbed the steps and did as I did the day before. I knocked the door and shouted through the letterbox, "Pauline." To my amazement mother came and opened the door in quick time. I said thank you as I walked past her and went up into my room. No other words were exchanged between us for the rest of the day.

I was suffering and deep down I knew mum was too. I could see it was getting more and more difficult for her to cope with daily chores. Money was tight so all buying of any items seized. Many nights we went to sleep on an empty belly. Out of pure desperation at not having I took up a suggestion made to me by a friend. "If you don't take what you need Shavon, then who's going to give it to you." I started to mix with a group of girls that knew all about taking what you want and not having to pay for it. The only snag was if you got caught, you'd get a criminal record and possibly get sent to prison. A price I did not consider when faced with personal need. I learnt that an integral part of survival amongst the have-nots was shoplifting and boy could they shop lift.

Mother rarely asked where I got things from but when she did, I'd just say Cecile, or my aunties gave it to me, which always seemed to do the trick. For a short while I used my new craft for emergencies only, for example if I had no food or my shoes were worn. But it wasn't long before I broke those boundaries and started to enjoy the adrenalin buzz it gave. Like an aphrodisiac the high of acquiring gave me a sense of control over my life that I didn't have and provided me with the essentials I couldn't afford.

However, in the back of my mind I always knew that, that wasn't the route for me. I didn't want it to become an excuse of necessity because I had, had a hard life. It bothered me that I was creating yet another escape route filled with disaster from my already disastrous life. At school I was the, "Have a laugh Shavon," at home the, "Introvert

Billy no mates" and on the weekends, "Thief." It was doing my head in because all I wanted was to be me, I just didn't know who me was anymore. I prayed for things to get better whilst secretly keeping my mouth shut.

Thanks Be To The Father

The year was soon to become the past when mother decided that she would turn to the church. She had also started to drive her blue Beetle again having stopped for the best part of the year. I was all for it if it helped. We used to attend Baptist prayer meetings on a Fridays in a house in Clapton. A man and his wife held the sessions. The men and women both wore white gowns, but the women had to cover their heads. Everyone wore different color bands, which they wore around their waist that symbolized their rank in the church. The wife's name evades me, but I always remembered the man. Everybody called him Father.

They were a Nigerian family. They had two daughters and a son. I really warmed to father; he had the calmness of the rising sun about him that made me feel relaxed. He would receive messages from the divine one and ask if anyone wanted to see if there was a message for them to come forth. Often, I would find myself kneeling before him and often he would say with a smile, "Don't worry, everything will be fine." The adults would be in one room and the children in another. When it was a full house, everybody just jammed together and when father handed the collection plate amongst the congregation, everybody dug deep to put towards the new church yet to come.

I liked going there, I had made many new friends that genuinely made me laugh besides, it was a comfort to have people who hardly knew me pray for my wellbeing. I could see it was making a difference to mum too. Without fail every Friday she made sure we were there. I guess in the nucleus of her madness a piece of mum was still fighting to be whole, trying to find the lost pieces of her life that seem non-existent in the reality she lived. Maybe she too like me, felt a sense of belonging, a feeling of relief and release that finally she could take some of her hearts cargo and place it at the feet of the Almighty who is known to be merciful and just.

For the first time I felt needed and I believed mum did too. We had both been let down by life's imperfections and had lost hope in what our eyes could see for often they had deceived us. In the mid-flow of discovering the Creator, the all-knowing, like children we were beginning to find ourselves.

The cycle of, "Same old, same old," was starting to break away and be replaced with something I wanted to look forward to, hope. I was curious about faith and that feeling of spiritual inner comfort I received in knowing, that this God was restoring what no man could. I was seeing the changes before my eyes and it brought light into my heart causing my frozen tears to thaw.

Coming to a place of worship planted the seed of

community and belonging, you are not alone. No matter how crap my week was, there was always Friday's to look forward to and even though my problems didn't go away, I guess my hearts confusion was replaced with optimism and understanding if not for just a while. It didn't mean I wasn't still angry at life, it just meant I wasn't as angry as I used to be. I became more determined to help mum get right for I had seen that there was something worth living and fighting for.

It was not long before Father had acquired a church in Elephant and Castle. I remember it as if it were yesterday. It was a Friday night service and Father had said the last amen, amen and then he announces to everyone we have a church. The house erupted with excitement, laughter, joy and plenty amen thereafter. The amount of noise and carry on that took place that day, you would have thought some big rave was going on. Indeed, we were raving with praises to the Most High. At long last prayers had been answered, a church had been provided. A piece of me was going to miss meeting up in the house. There was something about being cramped in a room with people virtually sitting on your lap that I enjoyed. You had no choice but to make conversation and run two joke.

When God chose that church, he supplied a congregation consisting of fitters, carpenters, plasterers, seamstresses, chefs, accountants, doctors, lawyers and artists. I'm sure there must have been one of every kind in this seemingly small group of people that just wanted to serve the Lord. One by one they came forward to offer their services to prepare the church for opening. Mum put me and herself forward to help clean the church too. God was truly grabbing a hold of mum for she behaved more normally at church than anywhere else. I thought the days of mum making friends and having a laugh was truly over but, being in this church broke the mold. I felt blessed in the little hope that glimmered through the mud. It's funny but for the first time I looked forward to doing a bit of hard work and getting my hands dirty.

There were designated days for people to come into the church and clean. I've never seen so much rubbish, pile upon pile, corner to corner and that was just the upstairs. There was dust everywhere and not a clean place to sit. Yet I was I happy covered in dirt from head to toe proudly displaying the scratches and scrapes of my labour. Every evening after a cleaning up, we would meet in the basement where the women would dish up the food they had prepared earlier. Boiler chicken and jaloff rice with a carton of orange juice. It was great, because the smell of the food on the fire with the sounds of children laughing and mums giving out orders or dishing up punishments felt like home.

This church thing was turning out to be alright. I can't say I grabbed a hold of religion or even deep knowledge of the bible, I just knew this was a place where I felt a sense of piece, joy, understanding and an awakening to a higher source that could change things no man could.

My rejection was being replaced with acceptance and helplessness restored to faith. It didn't seem to vex or embarrass me so much when mum had her off days, for I knew watching eyes were seeing with understanding. They'd always give me that look of, "I feel it for you man," and then they'd ask me, "Are you all right?" which I'd always reply with, a nod of the head and a raise of an eyebrow. This group of people who became our friends accepted us. We weren't judged or looked down upon indignantly for our imperfections because let the truth be known, everyone had some deep-rooted problem. Never the less, no matter how

65

many steps back or forward mum took, she was definitely showing signs of finding the will to beat her depression, Pauline didn't seem to surface so much.

Finally, the day had come for the opening of the church. I was so excited as I hadn't seen inside for about a week or so and was desperate to see the final transformation. A mass of people had arrived early all shining and gleaming in their Sunday best, buzzing around waiting for Father to arrive to lead us in. Not before long he arrived in a mint blue Royals Royce with his family and relatives. He was a humble man, but I know he felt proud that day. I could see the excitement in his face as his flock greeted him. With his back held straight and a massive grin on his face, he walked towards the church gates. His gown-radiated a brilliant white, whilst his ocean blue band around his waist embroidered in a yellow cross said let us begin.

Inside, the church was beautifully decorated with flowers and fruit whilst the atmosphere breathed frankincense and mire. As you enter the church hall all you see is a long isle that is carpeted in a rich ocean blue that leads to a humongous alter above which sits a massive cross. Even the foyer was big. Women on their period would have to sit there during the prayer sessions. It was forbidden to enter the church when you were unclean. Situated downstairs in the basement where the toilets, the kitchen and a very big hall with loads of different exits, a child's perfect playground. Often after the sermon myself and a few of the other children would gather there and play.

Church introduced me into many things and many people, in particular a boy called Justin. Justin was partially deaf, and he had to wear a hearing aid. His speech was slightly impaired so at times, I would find it hard to understand what he was saying. Most of the time, I didn't, I just made out I did so I could be near him for a while and have my true feelings go undetected. The truth is I found his indifference intriguing and fancied him incredibly from the first moment I saw him. I used to get tingles in my body when Justin would just look at me. Every girl that was young enough in the congregation fancied Justin. He was a black Caribbean, slim build, thirteen-year old boy with a small Afro who always looked slick in his clothes.

He was so boisterous and often got into trouble with his mum at church, I guessed that's why I liked him he was different. I had never fancied a boy before that made me feel over whelmed just by looking at them. I always considered boys mates and found playing Shavon the tomboy much easier to fit in. I wasn't into doing the girly stuff like showing feelings and writing I love you letters, I'd rather hide in the shadows and watch them from a distance feeling like a complete prat. The funny thing was Justin only fancied white girls.

The time was drawing near, and I was soon to be fourteen but not quite there yet. Everybody in church seemed to be putting his or her name down on a list to be baptized. I asked mum if I could be baptized too and she agreed. I was having my own personal white gown and hat made for me. I would wear the band of yellow that signified being ordained into the church and officially becoming a church member.

The whole church was buzzing with activity in the preparation of Baptism. The women elders were preparing the food and the church hall with flowers and fruit. The scent of frankincense and mire which I couldn't stand for so long, I now loved, and it filled the entire church. I felt proud and ready to receive the Lord into my life and I knew it would make my mother happy. If anything, I thought it might give her some strength.

The day had finally arrived, everything had been prepared, the church, the food and all the gowns. I was ready. The baptism took place in a small swimming pool which was situated in the back of the church. I remember there was a cross in the middle of the pool swirling around and around. It looked amazing. I kept thinking, "How did they do that?" Father was in the pool with his helper all dressed in white. We all stood against the wall whereby one by one we were summoned to enter the pool to be baptized and then it was my turn. As strange as it sounds, even though I had seen others baptized before me, I still did not know what to expect.

Father looked at me and with soft eyes and a smile he signaled for me to come forth. As my toes entered the pool, I took a quick gasp of air because the water was cold. The helper took my right hand as father took my left. Holding me firm but not tight they started to pray for me and with an, "Amen," they submerged me under water for about two seconds and I arose baptized.

As I made my way out of the pool, I felt refreshed and clean. I felt an immense sense of inner contentment and wanted to do it all over again. I didn't want to lose the sensation of being protected and having my slate wiped clean. I knew a special moment when I felt one because I had lost so many. This day was a special moment.

After the sermon and plenty amen, there was music, dancing, children playing, laughter, chitter chatter and plenty eating. The atmosphere was one I had secretly longed for in my own life. The presence of harmony and togetherness engulfed your air space that made you feel at peace with your neighbour. There was nothing but joy and good tidings to be gat. Like God's love, it came in abundance and filled everyone's belly. The sentiment of being at one with oneself over flowed in everyone's cup that day. There was more than enough love to go around and it felt good to share that with people who cared and understood. It was certainly one of the happiest occasions spent in my life.

Several months had passed and all was well when out of the blue one evening, whilst mum was driving home from church carrying passengers all huddled up in the back seat and myself sat in the front, I felt a shift in the energy. I kept looking at her because I noticed that her facial language had begun to change, I could sense that trouble was brewing. That was the look of Pauline, she had never surfaced at church, but tonight she was going to make an exception, she was making a début appearance with her bitchy self. As Pauline grabbed a hold becoming the dominant force a look of, "I don't won't you here," besieged her face and that's when her driving became erratic.

She kept stopping and starting, sharply jerking the passengers that were already overcrowded in the back, backward and forward, but no one dared say a word apart from, "Oops." I watched their eyes flicker from left to right in silent panic as mother drove over every bump and blemish in the road with a vengeance. I prayed we'd reach their destination speedily for I felt so embarrassed at the thought they might actually die with me because of my mum's actions. It was a blessing they were all getting off at the same stop.

When we arrived at the drop off point, they all hurried out of the car like ants as they said there secret, thank God goodbyes. By this time mum was totally entrenched in her zone of Pauline, perplexities were written all over her face. She did not utter a word neither did she look left or right. All I could do to appease their concerned expressions was give, a Laurel and Hardy look, as mum took off with speed into the night, screeching down the road like a lunatic.

I was glad that they were gone. The weight of their thoughts digging into my back that made me feel like I had a hump was far too heavy for me to carry. I could only straighten up when I knew they were out of my sight. The rest of our journey home was continued in silence just as it had started. That was the last time we went back to church or saw our friends again. Mother was hatching new plans.

My Father's House

Out of the blue mother decides she's going back to Jamaica for a few weeks. This was not a shock to me as mum had often traveled in her past. However, she had not traveled alone since her nervous breakdown. I really wanted to go with her, but I was in the middle of doing my mock exams and did not want to return home only to re-sit them again, so I decided to stay behind.

Mum didn't want me to stay in the house alone, so I had to stay with my grandparent's until she returned. She had given me the child benefit book and I was to give my grandmother something like eight or ten pounds a week. I had the keys to the house and had to hold the fort until she came back. I was worried sick about her leaving. It was the not knowing if the love of humanity would prevail in them far away planes and if it would lend a helping hand if my mother were to fall. Not only that, I was fearful of entering the house alone. How was I going to cope?

When mum eventually left destined to Jamaica, I pined for her for days to return. I pined because I missed her, I pined because I still felt alone, and I pined because as much as I loved my grandparents, I didn't want to live with them. For a short while everything was running relatively smoothly. My bedroom was at the top of the house beside my aunt Sybil's room. I had my own space and spent a lot of time in it by myself. My grandparents meant well but I don't think they truly understood neither did they have the time to address what I had gone through. They still thought I was their little granddaughter who always did as she was told and gave no backchat.

I had always remembered grannies as the place to be. The family unit that was tighter than tight. The family name with all its connections spread too many regions. Many people knew me even though I didn't know them, it was like that. What once was a place of sanctuary to me was no longer. All I felt was restricted, reduced to being a child I had wanted to be for so long, but no longer was. I had clutched onto past childhood memories that did not live up to my expectations in my here and now and it made me resentful towards them. I started to give trouble.

Before I knew it, my grandparent's and I were at my dad's house. I had not seen my father's face for the best part of six or seven years. I wondered what he could possibly have to say after all, he abandoned me too. They were discussing whether my father and his wife Averill could take me in. They were talking about me as if I wasn't there. I remember looking scornfully at my grandmother and my grandfather catching my eye and sharply telling me, "Take that look of your face before I wipe it off." Between them, they decided that I would go and stay with my father's that coming weekend. This gave me two days to pack.

After that, I said nothing more to my grandparents until I was ready to leave. I remember packing all that I could carry into plastic bags and a little wooden woven suite case that belonged to my aunt Sybil. My granddad was in the sitting room and my grandmother was in the kitchen. I never bothered to ask my granddad for a lift, I just said goodbye to him and as I walked out the front door, I shouted goodbye to my grandmother who was in the kitchen. I do not remember hearing her reply, just as I don't remember waiting for an answer. As I shut the front door behind me, I thought right, let's see how long this one will last.

I felt no lasting pain as I walked away, it was more of a whatever type feeling. Like a bag lady, I got on the 73-bus forward bound to fathers or, "Fitzs," as I called him. Fitzs was the father of my brother Nicky and I. Cecile had a different dad who we never knew. Apparently, when mother came to England as a teenager, she struck up a relationship with an older man and fell pregnant with Cecile. Her mother, mamma Sarah and stepfather, Mr. Clayman decided to press charges against this man for having sex with a minor. He was convicted whereupon he was sent to prison. Well, that was the story we were told. It did not make a difference to me who Cecile's dad was because she would always be my sister. However, it did make a difference to mum as I noticed she treated Cecile differently from Nicky and me.

I never really saw mum give her affection or shower her with gifts. As a small child not knowing any better, I took advantage of the advantages that came my way for my own selfish gain. That meant getting the upper hand on my sister at all times where and when possible. The name of the game between siblings in our house was, blackmail and getting away with shit. Cecile and Nicky weren't so smart when it came to the, knowing how to behavior in order to get what you want department, so my armory was forever full of ammunition. It was only years down the line that Cecile revealed her true feelings about growing up. She told me that she hated me when I was younger as I was spoilt. Upon reflection I agreed but to hate me? My love for her was constant even when she was getting on my nerves and I assured her of that.

Still sat on the bus with all that I could muster, thoughts of my absent father flooded every corner of my mind. I recollect being a toddler when my father took my brother and I out for a ride in a white van he used to have. He always wore a camel coat, which I believe he has up to this very day. My brother and I would take turns sitting on his lap at the driver's wheel whilst he drove around the flats where we lived.

I always remember having great feelings of love and not tolerating a bad word being said against him. However, like magic, with a puff of smoke and a wave of a wand, the thoughts and feelings I'd so dearly clung to as a child had disappeared with age. All that remained was questions of why? Why did it take a crisis to bring us together?

My dad married Averill in 1973 when I was three and Nicky was four years old. I had seen the wedding photos at my grandmother's house. I had two younger half-brothers Eze pronounced eh-zeh meaning King and Fathi pronounced fah-thee meaning victorious, who I did not particularly like at the time, I'm not sure why. Not long after dad was married, he had an extra marital affair with a woman called Claudette producing three more children. There were two girls and one boy who were slightly younger than the first batch so, then there were seven. Later on, an eighth child was to join the already extended family on Averill's side, my little brother Tayari pronounced tah-yah-ree. I don't know what record my dad was trying to set but he was definitely going for gold whatever it was.

It was weird to think that for so many of these years I'd wondered where and what my dad might be doing only to find out that he's been living a twenty-minute bus ride from where I lived, I was not impressed. I had placed him on a pedal stall for so long and he no longer matched those images, everything fell short. It was easier to cope with his absence when I thought he lived far away, at least then I could live in hope. But no, not my life, I must see things for exactly what it is, it is my destiny.

When I arrived at dads with all my baggage, Averill greeted me at the door. I had brief memories of Averill when I was about five or six years old. They weren't particularly pleasant. Before they moved to Leyton, they used to live on Holly Street at the back of Dalston. Averill had asked me to do something. I'm not sure if I refused or made a facial expression at my discontent, all I remember was her big fat hand connecting with my face and me running into the toilet crying how much I hated her and wanting to go home never to return. And here I was at her door once again but now as a young lady.

I had done a lot of growing since then and desperately wanted to settle down and live a family life. I had enough of struggling and doing it on my own. I put aside my past memories of dislike and consciously made an effort in my mind, that this time around would be a fresh start. As I walked into the house in Belmont Park Road, I headed towards the kitchen were Averill was packing out her shopping. She sat me down at the dining table and proceeded to give me a prep talk on how things were going to be.

It all sounded impressive. The living arrangements were that I'd share a room with my two brothers until proper space could be arranged for me. The journey to school was going to be a bit longer than usual but it did not really bother me. Between myself, her and my brother Eze, we would share the household chores. If there were any problems, I could just go and talk to her about it. She knew I had been through a lot with my mum and that things would take time to heal. "Everything's going to be alright okay," I remember her saying that as she rubbed my back.

I felt so welcomed and wanted by her, I actually believed every word she said. I really thought this was going to be a fresh start for me. I thought this would give me an opportunity to get to know my father as I had long since forgotten him. Within days of settling in I was missing mother's presence.

Word had reached me via one of my mother's old-time friend, Charles, that she was having difficulty in Jamaica. I didn't know what to do, not only that I hadn't visited the house for at least three weeks. I decided that I would have to put my fears of the house being alive aside and check that everything was alright, as no one else was going to do it for me.

So, one day after school, I decided to visit my sister Cecile and then check on the house on the way back to my fathers. After I left my sisters flat, I could feel the anxiety building up inside of me ready to freak out into flip mode at any given moment. Whilst taking deep breaths to steady my nerves, I kept reminding myself, "You are just going in and then coming out." It was as if I was enacting a scene from a movie. Except, I had no choice in the matter of the role I had to play. I was the dumb, poor, innocent girl, entering a spooky derelict house all on her own, knowing full well that something is not right, yet I still enter as I call out, "Is anybody there," as I shut the door behind me.

Doing a very good impression of when wonder women pissed herself, I arrived at the house confronted with an over whelming sensation that something or someone was looking out of my bedroom window watching me. They knew I couldn't see them, but they knew I could feel their presence. I thought, "Shit!" Knowing I had no choice but to go in I put on a brave face. As I opened the door, I shouted out, "Whose there? You better get out now." The house was so quiet. If there were a pin dropping, I would have heard it. I knew the house was empty of people it was just that, something else, that bothered me.

The quietness breathed beware, the walls and ceilings really do have ears and eyes. I do not recall hearing passing traffic in the street, or even children running a mock as school had not long ended. Not even the sounds of the birds singing do I recall. The atmosphere became motionless to me once I entered the house.

As I shut the door behind me, I walked up the stairs to the first landing. The back door had been broken in. "Oh my God," I shrieked, as I clasped my head with both hands feeling a complete and utter failure in not carrying out my mother's wishes of holding the fort. "We've been burgled." Streams of tears ran down my face as thoughts of, "Mummy is going to kill me," ran through my mind. Not only had I let strangers come into our home and violate the little we had left, there was also no electricity or hot water. No one mentioned to me about paying any bills, I was only fourteen and a half, I hadn't even started my period yet, what did I know about house-keeping.

I felt so disappointed in myself for not being stronger and overcoming my fears. My conscious kept telling me, "You've really let your mum down this time and she's never going to forgive you." Why does it always seem when you are trying to do good that the devil plagues you more? Forever putting obstacles in your way for you to trip and fall.

The thieves had stolen my mother's eight-seated solid wood, dining table and chairs. They also stole her stereo tucked away in the back of her wardrobe. I don't know how the thieves missed the records, as they too were at the back of the wardrobe but, thank God they didn't anyway. They had also rummaged through my chest of draws and left all my clothes on the bedroom floor. The fact that strangers roamed my house, not knowing what they had touched or what they did made me feel defiled. Overcome and distraught I secured the back door the best I could and headed towards my sisters. I was afraid the thieves would come back to claim the lasts of my mother's things. I had to think fast to salvage and secure what I could.

I asked my sister if she could take mum's records, the one thing that had survived her break down. She agreed and came back to the house and took them. I returned back to my dad's and told him what had happened. I suggested that we needed to go back to the house as quick as possible and get my bed and the rest of my clothes. Within a few days my father, Eze and me returned to mums to collect the rest of my things. It was clear to me that whoever had come to the house before had been back. I could not get it out of my mind the shock that mother might go through when she came back home to its new state. My heart sank as I cried my invisible tears.

When my brother and father entered the house, I remember a shocked expression on their faces. My father looked at me with repented eyes, yet he said nothing apart from, "Let's get the things packed into the van." I must have entered into the world of myself after that for a few days. If it was not one thing it was always another. To top it all off I had also lost the house keys. What was I going to do? On one hand, I was missing mum and concerned for her safety desperately wanting her to come home, but on the other, I was riddled with fault and shame that when mum did come back to find her home ransacked it would make her condition worse, a fire I had fueled with my carelessness. There was nothing left for me to do but wait for her return and face the consequences.

Back at dad's house I settled into the spare room, which was a love hate affair. It was great to finally have my own space however, it was linked to an adjoining bathroom, if only it wasn't the main bathroom. Every morning as Averill got up for work at about six o'clock, she would come hurdling into the room swinging the doors open like she wanted to take the hinges off as she'd stomped, crash, bang, wallop straight through to the bathroom. It sounded like a heard of elephants on speed. I thought, "Has she ever considered that perhaps I might be sleeping and just maybe take her time and walk a bit lighter on her feet?" No chance. I felt she was doing it on purpose just to wake me up, even though I always pretended I was asleep.

Frustrated with my environment I was finding it increasingly difficult to breathe at my dad's, especially having the wicked witch from the east as a stepmother who was determined to convert me into this little girl whom she always wanted, who was clearly showing signs of resistance. I was doing all the laundry, majority if not all the ironing. I was finding her to be bossy, spiteful, smothering, over bearing and wanting to control everything and everyone in the house just because she had no control over my father.

The honeymoon period was defiantly over for me and that fresh start we were supposed to be having, well that turned into something we hadn't discussed. As for my dad, he was absent when I was not living with him and absent when I was. My views had changed towards the idea of family life in a household that by no medical default was naturally loveless.

Two Bulls in One Pen

Averill was a very angry woman who loved my father more than she loved herself. She sacrificed self-love with all her dreams and aspirations to land second place even though, "She name wifey." She tolerated his marital affairs and endless children, settling for lonely nights, all for my father's last name. One night my dad suggested to Averill he'd take her out, something I rarely saw him do. They were going to roll in a van with a group of sound men to get into the dance. Naturally she was excited, I thought, "Finally, if he pays her some attention then it will take the heat off of mine and Eze back, at least for a couple of weeks." I was smiling. But the course or true love never runs smoothly.

As Averill glided towards her wardrobe to examine her wears Fitzs turns to me and says, "Why don't you come?" Automatically, a frozen scene was created which lasted all of half a minute of Averill looking at dad scornfully from the corner of her eye, dad looking at me seemingly oblivious to the daggers Averill was throwing in his back and me looking at Averill with that plastic smile that said, "Never mind." Needless to say, she was not too thrilled about it and to be honest neither was I, but I felt put on the spot, so I said, "Yes I'll come."

As we set off on our journey there were pure good vibes in the van, everyone was laughing, and I genuinely believed we were really going to have a good time until my father said, he had to do one more stop and pick up. Father never told us he had invited anyone else. But when we saw whom dad had stopped off to pick up, Averill's smile became permanently removed. We had stopped off to pick up Claudette. Now I understand why he wanted me to come.

Any spec of joy Averill had concerning the night out had been totally disbanded. I couldn't believe he'd be so blatant and bold. But then again, it was not like Claudette was a secret, everybody knew, and it wasn't the first time we'd been to functions and she was there. Averill must have felt like crap, but she seemed to play the wife status remarkably well and maintained her composure with civility.

He walked around so proud in the dance that night in his red, gold and green crown with matching belt. He greeted his friends, "Iree," grinning from ear to ear as his hair bobbed up and down. He must have felt like an African king with three beautiful queens by his side knowing two of them where his main squeeze. Whatever imperfections Averill had, she didn't deserve to be treated like that. She wasn't the socialite/intellectual type like Claudette, but she could cook a mean dinner and have any house sparkle from top to bottom. Most of all she really did love my dad.

Averill was hell bent on being the dutiful wife to a not so dutiful husband till death do she part. She was hell bent on maintaining that status even though she knew it was driving her to the brink of madness and that madness was trickling down to us, the children and it was making my life a living hell.

Father too spared no thought to the price others would have to pay for the choices he made. In my mind I saw it as he was too afraid to confront his heart's desires, so he forfeited his ideal of true happiness in exchange for a living sleep. This generated very little time to bond with him. As far as I was concerned, they both wagered love for right or wrong and lost and it showed in the family dynamics.

Every day after school my brothers and I would have chores to do before Averill came home from work, which we did. We would do our homework and then settle down to watch television. However, for some reason every time my brother's heard Averill's key in the front door they would jump out of their skin and start cleaning what they knew they had already cleaned. I would always get annoyed with them for doing that and tell them to sit down and relax but they never listened.

I suppose they knew their mother best, for from the very moment Averill entered the house after work, she entered like a raging bull in a china shop calling us out one by one to come and clean this and to sweep that. Occasionally she would hurl her fists that always seemed to connect in your back. This was particularly so for my brother Eze. It must have been a blessing when I came along as he was doing practically everything in the house.

He liked my rebelliousness and no fear attitude towards his mother, as did my brother Fathi. I never hid my feelings from them about how I felt about their mother, my step mum. They knew I wanted out of the house and I would frequently tell them, "I don't live here I'm just a lodger passing through." They'd always laughed when I said that and then my brother Fathi, who was born on the same day as me would say in response, "If I want to leave home can I come and stay with you," which I'd always reply, "Yes." I started to really bond with my brothers and knew if at any time that I would have to leave, I would miss them.

As days turned into months, the relationship between Averill and I started to wane. My patients had grown thin and my attitude towards the family set up had started to change. We were having major conflicts. I hated the way she would always try to embarrass my brothers and me when she had visitors over. Without fail a multitude of household tasks would miraculously appear that discerned immediate attention. I made the mistake once of inviting my best mate Chanika over. I don't know what I was thinking, be normal I guess, but after that experience I vowed never to do it again. That woman had chores coming out of my backside. The only time I had to talk to Chanika was when I was saying goodbye to her at the front door. She told me later that she wrote in her diary how she sorry felt for me and that my step mum was wicked.

Averill could be very theatrical when she gave us orders for others to bear witness. She took pride in letting us, the children know that she had the arsenal to humiliate us at anytime, anyplace and anywhere. As a direct result of Averill's unpredictable behavior that was becoming increasingly predictable, my brothers and I never brought friends home. The possibilities of what could happen were just not worth the risk. When we had guests over, I tried to stay out of her way which was virtually impossible because she had a way of being in your face even when you couldn't see her.

When there wasn't guest's, life with Averill and her emotions were based on what my father did or didn't do. These feelings were intensified when he'd be gone for days. There's a saying that you hurt the ones closest to you, but this was getting ridiculous. I wasn't a counselor but even I knew Averill's interaction with her children was a mirror image of the relationship between her and my dad.

One Friday Averill came home from work with all the shopping in a foul mood as usual, but this time, she had bought a girlfriend home with her. I just knew something embarrassing was going to happen but not even I could have predicted the embarrassment would be on Averill. She started calling names, "Eze, Fathi," do this do that. I was already in the kitchen with her and her friend packing out the shopping. For some reason Averill decided to turn her unwanted attentions on me and began to ridicule me to her friend about my incapability's to cook rice. In her moment of glory to shame me she neglected to see that her friend was not marveling in her tease.

She kept looking at me in that, "I feel sorry for you," look and I know all about that look like the back of my hand. She then turned to Averill as if frustrated with her banter and calmly said, "So what if she can't cook rice, not everybody can." She had risen to my defense, there is a God. I briefly looked at Averill with a smirk on my face. "Ya bitch you," this one's not playing your game of torment the children. I could see she was deeply perplexed by being corrected in front of me just as I knew, I would have to pay for my insubordinate smirk. Averill didn't miss a trick.

Shortly after her friend left all hell broke loose. Still in the kitchen, Averill decided to pick up a plate that I had washed the day before and tells me to look at it. As I looked at that plate, she pointed out that, it still had rice on it. With this, she took the plate and smashed it over my head at which point I steamed straight into her throwing as many punches as possible saying, "I hate you, I hate you, you're not my mum." I knew that would hurt her to her core, so I made sure I said it as loudly as possible as I ran upstairs into my room.

How dare she I thought, my father has never raised his hand to me before so what gives her the right. What if that plate had seriously cut me in my head? What would she have told my family and the doctors, "Oh she deserved it because the plate I washed still had a bit of rice on it." Fueled with gasoline ready to ignite with the littlest of spark, I knew I would not be staying another night in that house. My father came home not long after but said nothing to me apart from, "Iree." I knew Averill hadn't told him about what had happened and frankly I wasn't bothered. Regardless whether he knew or not, nothing and no one was going to stop me from leaving.

Later that night when the whole house was asleep, I rolled a few belongings in my sleeping bag, set it upon my back like puss in boots and climbed out the sitting room window securing it the best I could behind me. The night felt cold and unfamiliar to me. I felt afraid and dreaded the long walk down Lea Bridge Road. It was the type of road come nightfall, it changes into a desolate waist land that somehow generates that feeling that you're being watched. Any screams would be lost in the vast amount of openness that was never apparent during the day. Never the less, still determined with all my fears, I continued my journey.

As I reached the top of the high street, something told me to look down. As I did so, I caught sight of something small that lay perfectly camouflaged on the floor. As I reached down to pick it up, I could see it was a small beige leather purse no bigger than the palm of my hand. When I looked inside, I found five pounds and change. "God be praised," I said allowed. I knew he was watching over me and even though I had no home to go to as such, at least I had money. As quick as I had found the purse, I saw a 38-bus coming down the road heading in the direction of home so, I quickly jumped on it. For a while I forgot that I was running away and felt saved from the dreaded long walk.

Not before long I landed at my sister's place. Before I even got there, I knew my sister could not take responsibility for me as sure as I knew at some point I would have to go back to my dad's. So, I thought, let me use this short time to get close to, "MY FAMILY," even if it was frayed at the edges. I explained to my sister what had happened, and she said I could stay over for the weekend. I recall her listening a lot and offering me her sympathy but never an alternative. I felt subtly rejected, entwined with an immense sense of compassion for her. Her life embroiled with motherhood, violence and fear had changed her from the way I once knew and remembered.

Cecile was always tough and unafraid to speak her mind or fight any man or woman, respect was due however, like waves crashing against the beach shore, mighty rocks that once stood for years wear down, changing shape little by little, piece by piece until reduced to sand. So too had Cecile's toughness been altered, taking on a new appearance of something hardened and cold. She had the amazing ability to endure sufferation without showing signs of pain, as if it were water off a ducks back.

Determined in her quest not to let anyone in ever, she created her own safe place in her head, except this safe place was not safe at all. It was risqué and damaging to her real quality of life. Cecile had turned to crack for comfort, the devils pass time that quickly proceeded on to heroin, and then to a life, I am sure she herself could have never foreseen.

The weekend was nearly over, and I knew I had to leave my sisters at some stage especially, if I was going to go back to school the Monday. I hadn't spoken to my dad over the weekend in fact, I hadn't spoken to anyone about anything. With no fear of consequences, mid Sunday afternoon I strolled back in at my dad's. Averill had called my father to let him know that I had returned. As he came in, he said nothing to me. He just headed straight towards Averill, who was in the kitchen. As I sat on the stairs with my brothers, we listened to him cuss and curse, threatening to leave her. "No Fitzs, no Fitzs," she kept saying. I prayed secretly he would walk out taking me with him but, he never did.

He's a coward, I thought. He's too afraid to step into the unknown, so he'd rather play it safe whilst making everyone's life a living misery. This installed within me an outlook of dislike towards him, for from the beginning I was aware that my father was never around and the only person picking up the tab for his shortcomings was his wife who was as equally resentful because of his abandonment. I could not imagine being with a man, cooking for him, cleaning for him, washing his clothes, raising his family, accepting his illegitimate children into my home only to face many lonely nights, knowing full well, he's lying in the arms of another women. As much as I disliked Averill, I could empathize with her. I remember seeing her diary and that first page read, God help me PLEASE.

I knew I was causing stress and I genuinely did not want to live in contention with her, I just didn't know how to love her. I was used to having family discussions where we would share our thoughts and feelings without fear of repercussions or receive praises of acknowledgement for efforts well done. I became disheartened in my expectations in what a normal family was supposed to be like. They never gave hugs or kisses, I never heard them whisper the words, I love you. Rewards seemed to be given with one hand and then taken away with the other. No amount of effort to do well seemed good enough. Affection appeared minimal and happiness desirable but not essential.

I tried reasoning with my dad about the situation. I thought I made it clear to him in an around about way that for this family thing to work, he needed to spend more time at home. His expression told me he knew what I was already talking about, as if he had, had the very same conversation with himself many times over, but like a runaway train, he could not stop what he had started, neither undo what he had created. I really wanted to have faith in his words, but the whole set up seemed hollow. I could not shake the feeling that he had resigned himself to, "But what can I do?" We reasoned for hours, but it felt like a moment to me. Unconvinced of his reassurances for change, I went to bed in hope that the next day to come would be a better one.

Unfortunately, that better day never came. I tried my best to avoid unnecessary confrontation with Averill but biting my tongue was never my strongest point. You could cut the resentment in the air between us and this became evidently clear on the day I started my period. I was no more than fifteen years and a bit when I went to the toilet and wiped myself only to see blood on the tissue. Not alarmed, I went to Averill quite calmly and told her that I had started my period.

Averill looked at me with squinted eyes as she often did that read, if you were mine then you would see and said, "Well, you're just going to have to use what's there." Now Averill was a big woman and only used super plus tampons. I was horrified that she could stoop so low. Regardless, I tried to do the right thing and took the super plus tampon and pushed it up my virgin as far as I could physically bear. Not truly comprehending that virgin, plus super plus tampon equals not going to work, the experience was a painful one that chafed. I took to using tissue after that.

From then on, I knew being a good little girl was not going to work in my favor in this house. So, after her act of spite I decided I would do my best to irritate her from then on. Averill would often say to me with clenched teeth, "You can twist your dad around your little finger you can." I knew she wasn't wrong but being the rebellious and determined sort not to be controlled by anyone less than my biological parents, I would just look at her straight in the eyes with a blank expression on my face that read, do you really think I care. It sounds cruel, but I took pleasure in her melancholy. I felt justified, as she had duped me into moving into her home on the premise that everything was going to be all right.

A year in of living at dads, I craved to be alone and snatched every moment I could which, generally ended up with me spending hours in the toilet. It was the one place that was purpose built for one person and the only place I could find excuses for spending hours alone. Father was still playing; now you see me, now you don't, Averill was still being a pain and mother had returned home from Jamaica.

Mother's return made me nervous, as I did not know how she was going to react, especially when she found out that I was no longer living with my grandparents. There was no gas or electricity in the house and burglars had stolen the little possessions she had chosen to keep. All I kept thinking is why is this happening to me and what the blazes am I going to do?

A few weeks later mother arrives unannounced at my father's door. Myself, my brothers and Averill were in the house at the time, my father had gone out somewhere as usual. As Averill opened the front door, I was standing at the top of the stairs directly facing the door and that's when I laid my eyes upon my mother's face. I felt shocked, nervous, surprised and scared all at the same time. Our stares reflected our desire to hold one another. Averill, held her ground, combat stance not taking her eyes off the ball, not an inch.

Mother had been gone the best part of a year which was slightly longer than I anticipated however, I must say, with all my previous inner panic attacks of how is she going to cope, she looked remarkably well. She had cut her hair short, changed her image and had gone Asian, which suited her. It was refreshing to see her face once again and gave me hope that maybe she was on the mend.

Without word of warning, mother tried to push Averill out of the way and make a grab for me. I froze whilst Averill reacted straight into restrain mode. I became distressed at seeing mum distressed and thought that Averill was going to hit her. I yelled out, "Don't hit her, don't hit her." Everything went into slow motion, Averill turned and looked at me, my mother had stopped fighting in mid flow and was also looking at me. Within seconds mother turned away and walked off.

As Averill shut the front door behind her, I remember looking at the front door and visualizing it as a big iron gate being slammed in my face blocking the ones I loved out and locking me in. A prisoner in my mind of my circumstances. I ran up to my room tormented with hurt that I had let her down yet again. I wanted to go back home but I was afraid. I couldn't be a hundred percent sure that mum was trying to grab me to take me back home or to break my neck for not taking care of her things.

Miserable and home sick I would often sit by myself and think am I destined to feel this way forever? I tried to block out what had happened and the fact I was missing mum terribly. Nothing seemed to shake my pain. This was not helped by the fact that mother had come up to my school one day asking to speak to me. I was walking through the playground on my way to a class, when a teacher approached me and said, "Your mother's in reception wanting to see you." I was assured that there would always be a teacher present however, like before I felt afraid of the, what ifs and rejected her. Why could I not see that mother was really trying? Maybe if I had gone to see her it might have helped the situation, but my mind was too focused on the state of the house and that no matter what she said she was definitely going to kill me.

I never saw my mum for quite a while after the incident during which time, I had been living at dad's for nearly two years. I had obtained my qualifications from school and was in college doing a Certificate in Pre-vocational Education that I was soon to finish. That's when my brother Nicky came to live at Averill's. At last I had an allied. Averill's presence didn't seem to bother me so much when he was around, and it took my mind off mum too. Having my brother around was refreshing, he reminded me of love once felt and I was keen for him to stick around. He made me feel safe to remember when we were young, adventurous and fearless. In his company I could be that little girl of ten and seek and gain comfort by just being by his side.

Again, I found myself wallowing in past memories to camouflage my present life however, in keeping with the current pattern of my life, which is nothing seems to stay around too long, Nicky's stay was to be a short lived one. When he left so did all the good memories and fun times. It felt like he was leaving me all over again as in the beginning to fend for myself. I was wrapped up in the pit of nothingness that paved over the cracks and cast a constant shadow over my one true thought, my one true missing link to home. I went into a state of mourning.

As plain as a piece of paper I tried the best I could to tolerate my environment and get on with my life. Occasionally on the weekends I would visit my sister. It seemed to disjoint Averill that I had a life outside of, "The family." She would always try and put obstacles in my way when I wanted to go. Sometimes she'd pushed me too far, and I'd reach that place where my facial expression and steer would communicate, "Say I can go, or I'm going anyway, and then you can explain it to my dad," at which point she would style it out for me to go, like, I really needed her permission to see my sister.

For respite to get out of the house, I decided to take up trampolining at our local youth club. I was always good at it at secondary school and really enjoyed it. I believed at the time it would help me to divert my energy of, "I hate my life," into something positive. I didn't want to be the angry sister all the time. I wanted to feel completeness in my heart because I still yearned for its touch. So, me being me I thought, I'd give the trampoline thing ago and make an effort to gain some control over my rebelliousness, give everyone a break but more importantly, give myself one.

My brothers and I would go club every other week or two, well it was a hit or miss really, but I was glad that some activity was going on. We always had a good time even though there wasn't much to do. One fine day my brother Fathi was watching me trampoline and was very much impressed, as was the teacher, who thought I was good enough to enter competitions. I can't begin to tell you what those few words of encouragement did for my spirit, I was on high.

My brothers and I laughed and joked all the way home that evening, I couldn't wait to share the good news. When we arrived, we headed straight towards the kitchen where Averill was doing something or other. In my excitement I even forgot I was angry with her, I forgot she wasn't my mum and became that little girl who just wanted to sit and talk with her mum. It was with that type of thinking, that's she was able to leave me speechless.

She must have been hatching her moment to devour me for some time, more than likely for something I may, or may not have done properly last year. Averill was not one for letting a wrongful deed, in her eyes, go unpunished. She always had a way of getting you back especially when you least expected it. All she had to do was be patient and that she was.

When we arrived back at the house we headed straight to kitchen to let Averill know what had taken place. Everything seemed fine until my brothers went upstairs to wash up, leaving me alone in the kitchen with her. All alone she turned to look at me and with her mouth twisted to the left she said, "You ain't going anymore." I could hear the knife twisting between her teeth. As I think back, I don't remember her showing any enthusiasm or interest in what

94

we were saying. In fact, I don't recall her saying anything, not even "Oh, that's good well done."

She acted with such speed I had no time to defend myself from her cutting words. All I knew was, I was wounded. She had seized the moment to crush me for all the crap I put her through in the past. Where not better to strike than at the desires of my heart, it was the last thing I needed to hear or feel. Completely stumped I had no come back. I hanged my head down and went upstairs to my room.

Thoughts of, "I have had enough of you, you bloody bitch," kept running through my mind. It was then I knew I was going to leave, but not run away as I did before like a thief in the night. I was going to walk out the front door the same way I had entered and nothing and no one was going to stop me. I let a couple of days pass before I decided to tell my father about what had happened between Averill as he wasn't showing no signs to approach me. I let him know it was time for me to leave.

He tried for hours to persuade me to change my mind. I explained to him that I was not happy living in his home. I was unhappy with the way Averill treated my brothers and me, I was unhappy with the fact he was never around when we needed him and for all the hours and years of talking and reasoning nothing ever seemed to change. I left him in no doubt that my decision was final, I was going back home to my mum's. This time I was going to solider out the weather and make it through the storm no matter what.

That night I told my brothers that I was leaving, their eyes filled with such sadness. I was sad that it did not work out yet happy that I had got to know them. My brother Fathi kept asking me, "If I want to leave home could I come and stay with you," which I'd always reply, "Yes." I was going to miss them, the fun times spent in the launderette when we would spend off some of the drying money on sweets or sitting at the dinner table trying to pinch each other's pieces of meat off the plate or trying to rub Vicks up one another noses or just purposely getting one another into trouble just to get a laugh. I had established new bonds with my younger brothers, and I encouraged them to be who they felt they were and not to be afraid to speak their minds. I knew they would never forget me likewise, I would never forget them.

The next day Averill summoned me into her bedroom. I could feel she was on the verge of exploding as she stood by the window in her nightdress folding clothes. The atmosphere felt tense and uninviting. As I stood at the bedroom door, she asked me why I was leaving. Her tone was sour and indignant. I just kept looking at her blankly for I knew the time for talk was done. I watched my silence creep under her flesh and irritate her jaw bone. As if plagued by her inner voice she persisted in saying, "Is it because of me, is it, is it, you can tell me." Yeah right, what could I possibly tell her that she didn't already know?

Could this be another one of her, "Trust me games," where she coxes you into this false sense of security for you to reveal all and then she turns around and consumes you with lyrics of the why's and therefore which doesn't work in your favor. I was not falling for it this time. We both knew the real reason behind this big decision, going back home was just a decoy from having to say, "I hate living here and I hate you."

It's strange, but I really didn't have a clue where I was going to go when I left will all my belongings. I hadn't seen or spoken to mum for quite some time. Filled not with enthusiasm at the thought of the reception I might get neither the likely hood of having to start from where I left off, I was leaving anyway.

After some time of interrogation, refusing to give anything more than my name, rank and number I eventually spoke and with a smug look on my face said, "I just want to go home." With that, Averill dismissed me from her bedroom looking somewhat distressed and frustrated by my lack of co-operation to tell her the truth, even though she already knew what the truth was.

Maybe she had to be sure because maybe I made her feel that she had somehow failed in her attempts to raise a girl child. As I walked to my bedroom, I felt victorious. I felt empowered and uplifted as I thought, "Gotcha." With all her efforts to break and reshape me into the girl I never was, I had won the battle. I had refused to be broken and controlled. I was sixteen and a pinch. I had finished sixth form by the skin of my teeth and now I was taking my freedom instead of waiting to be freed. I was going to make my own decisions from now on. How hard could it possibly be?

Smell the Coffee

Like the story of my life, chapter and verse, as one door shuts another one opens. The only problem with revolving doors is, you never really know where you're going to come out to. It's a game of Russian roulette. From the moment I shut the front door of Belmont Park Road behind me, I knew I was back in the world all on my lonesome as once before. Leaving dads paved the way towards liberty and taking control over my own life choices no matter how daunting and unpredictable it seemed.

Unsure of where I was really going with only doubt to look forward to, I ended up at my sister's doorstep. She took me in and made me feel welcome. My brother was living there at the time too which was a double bonus and I loved being around my niece Shantel. Finally, for the first time in many years I was living under one roof with my brother and sister, it felt like old times. I thought the weight of taking care of mum and myself would be lifted. How wrong was I?

Where my life experiences seemed to stop and start at mum, my brother and sister had moved on with their lives. Nicky was getting up to all kinds of insanities. Sometimes it was hard to know what was going on in his head. At times he was an extravert who thrived on attention with girls, girls everywhere and then he'd have moments of complete solitude immersed in thought. Deep down he was looking for a better life that offered understanding and wisdom and frequently he made attempts to know the Most High and live good, but the temptation of material splendor always seemed to have the upper hand. A heavy price he would later have to pay.

Cecile was still taking crack and heroin and becoming a different person on rapid. Like the fighter she is, she put on a brave front to defend her addiction to cover the rail tracks of hurt and abuse she had suffered from the hands of her daughter's dad who later turned out not to be. To me she had gone through some sort of metamorphosis transforming her from a beautiful butterfly into a grubby moth. I didn't recognize her anymore and worst still I didn't know how to deal with her. Cecile was venturing down a dark and slippery road, something I could never have imagined unless I had seen it with my own eyes. Slowly but surely loving my sister became very painful and I wasn't prepared for that.

In my bid to escape the frying pan, I had jumped into the fire of dreams that don't come true. It was strange to think I had wished for this moment for so long yet all it revealed was a familiar sadness. I had unearthed a reality I hadn't prepared for, that magnified my burden of responsibility. Not only was I worrying about my brother extra curriculum activity and the fact he could end up dead, I was also worried about Cecile who seemed to be losing all self-respect and care for herself and child. Then there was mum, whom we didn't often speak about apart from when we were reminiscing over old times.

After several months I found a job working in Camden as a Telephonist/Receptionist. It felt good to earn my own money for the first with the freedom to buy what I needed instead of having to steal it. I started to feel useful, like I had some control over my life. However, where one area of my life raises it seems another section falls. The good times that was meant to role, didn't role long for me.

It was hard to accept that we had entered new dimensions of our lives which propelled us into different directions. We were regressing back to children where arguments flared up over nothing, harsh words were said, fists were thrown, and tears were shed. It was hard to stay emotionally connected. Living together was becoming messy and chaotic. Disheartened that my bubble had burst, I became distant and eventually left to go and stay with my grandparent's once more.

Surprise, surprise it was short-lived. The same restrictions were applied even though I was working and paying my own way, well, practically. They didn't quite get it that I wasn't the little niece who was only interested in playing with pieces of material perched upon a clothes peg, as I marvel in its ability to sway like flowing hair that was not like mines. I was coming into my own space, and my family values had altered. I was defiant to the indoctrination of the ways of the past where you just keep your head down and grin and bear it.

My whole life had been about pretending and I was trying to break free from that. It wasn't healthy, and it didn't make sense. All it did was extend the life span of the hurt already afflicted and I was tired of feeling like the whipping boy. I learnt quickly from life experiences that whenever rocky times strike, I'm always left to myself having to hold the fort and fight the demons. It was evident that no one was going to save me or spare my feelings, so the only person I needed to rely upon, and trust was me and as long as I did that, I'd be fine.

Something needed to change so, armed with my pen I wrote down the pros and cons of the headaches I was getting at my grandparents and based on those results, I knew it was time for me to leave ASAP. I didn't want to reach the point where I couldn't hide my discontent and outwardly disrespect them but clearly my frustration was growing. So, I decided to leave and began my search for my own accommodation. Trying to find somewhere to live wasn't as easy as I thought it'd be. I made so many calls that day and received so many knock backs, but I was determined to persevere and succeed until eventually I found somewhere to go that day.

Everything was so black and white to me back then. If it wasn't this then it must be that, there was no in between. If I couldn't be accepted in one place, then I'd go to a place where I could. This didn't make me immune to rejection, quite the opposite but I'd learned to anticipate it and dodge its full blows. Leaving my grans would be like all those other times where I was thrown into the lion's den and left for dead yet someway, somehow, I'd make it through. It was time for me to spread my wings and fly.

After work I met up with my mate Chanika and we went to view a bed-sit in Stoke Newington. The house was clean and occupied about ten people of all ages. They seemed to be a lively bunch. The bedroom was shared, so was the bathroom and toilet. There was no kitchen but that was in the other house where a cook provided breakfast and all for sixty-four pounds a week. Based on what I had seen I accepted the room and went straight back to my grans to pack. I barely let the dust set beneath my feet as I gathered all my belongings and said my goodbyes. Within moments I was back at the hostel folding clothes into draws.

The first night was a sleepless one but it didn't take me long to settle in and make friends. I visited mum as often as I could and found living apart made our relationship exist in a much calmer place. She was always happy to see me and would often ask me to stay a little while longer when she knew I was just about to leave. She'd tell me stories of papers she had to sign, dues she had to pay and how tired she was. I continued to work for a while until out of the blue I was made redundant and found myself living foot loose and fancy-free on income support. How that novelty wore off quick.

I started to contemplate going back home. I knew mum was lonely and besides I was getting fed up with the bed-sit life, sometimes hungry until I'm weak or half-starved of company for weeks. Being Miss Independent wasn't all what it was cracked up to be. At least at home I could guarantee that someone would be there who truly needed me. Life can be so peculiar. Who truly understands what compels us to do the things we don't understand yet somehow, we are instinctively drawn through life's schizophrenic current to do them? Where does that come from?

I decided to tell my mum that I was coming back home, and it would seem in the nick of time. I knew something was up with mum from previous visits. She seemed to be displaying more emotion than normal. That was her usual way of communicating to me that something was wrong. For hours I would sit and talk to her, picking sense from nonsense to the point not even I knew what I was talking about. She always tried to hide her pain from me and appeared to keep things miraculously together with dignity and pride whilst secretly tripping out. Now I know where Cecile gets it from.

Whenever I trust my instincts, they always seem to steer me right. Mum was still causing pandemonium with the neighbours downstairs with her anti-social behavior, getting into trouble with all different types of authorities. Veronica a Scottish lady who lived in the flat below my mother's told me. She always kept me informed on what was going on whenever she saw me. Give thanks for Veronica, she never stopped caring. Alarm bells were ringing in my ears, as I knew that all this upset could result in mum being taken away from me once again and even possibly losing her home.

As panic started to set in, my scares of yester year started to ooze its puss. I was beginning to feel past guilt of the first-time mother was taken into hospital. One summers day I went to see her and after a few, "Pauline's" with no replies, Veronica comes along and says, "Six policemen came today and handcuffed your mum Shavon, and they threw her into the back of a police van and took her to Hackney Hospital. I was so upset Shavon, they didn't have to handle her like that." I was upset too but more so afraid for the fact that Stoke Newington Police had taken my mum. Apparently, mother had chased builders who were contracted by the council to do work on the front of the house down the road with a screwdriver.

It did not surprise me what mother had done yet it was still a blow to my system to be told that she was behaving that way. Clearly, she wasn't coping being alone. Up until that moment she had gone undetected in the system and those who did know did nothing. I too became accustomed to living without interference that made controlling my chaotic life a lot easier. However, now this had happened mum had exposed herself to the realms of the real world that was not so forgiving or compassionate.

Part of this exposure I felt was due to me, for I coveted a secret that nobody knew, not even mum. Several years previous when I was about fourteen years old, I went to the Social Services in Clapton Square in a last ditched attempt to get help for her. I couldn't shake the feeling that for my moment of gallantry, I gave Social Services privy information to store and use against my mum when and if they decided to play God in her life.

I remember the day like the cuts on my legs. I went to the Receptionist and said, "I would like to speak to someone about my mum please." I was placed in a dim room and told to wait whereupon an Asian man walked in with all these files in his hands. He wore abnormally big, brown, square glasses. His hair was short and jet-black with biggish wavy curls. He wore a dull beige shirt rolled up at the sleeves and a brown waistcoat with trousers to match, that looked a size too big to hide the fact that he was fat.

As I poured my heart out to this man, I never really saw him look at me or show compassion as I bared my soul, trying to be mature as I held back the dam of tears that filled my eyes. His face remained emotionless as I told my tragic story. All he kept doing was making these grunting sounds like a hog smelling the air, "Grunt, grunt." A moment came in between his grunting when he realized, I had stopped talking and was now just staring at him in utter disbelief. He sat up quick smart, looked me straight in the eye and said,

"I'm sorry but there's nothing we can do for you."

This man had consulted nobody, neither had he given advice as to the possible avenues I could take, and I was an underage child. Through his endless gaze out of the window on planet, "It's home time soon and I ain't got time for your shit little missy," he just kept checking his watch as he fiddled with his files with a fake, "Oh I'm sorry," smile on his face, until I made signs I was going to leave. With the little energy I had left, I managed to scrape my burnt out remains off the chair. As I made way for the door, he quickly shuffled behind me, one two, one two and with a superb half twist out, without touching, he squeezed past me disappearing behind a black door, "Bang." Bewildered and bemused just as I had entered, I had been thrown back out onto the streets with my words of help me, to carry my heavy heart in my hands and drink from the cup half empty of tears.

Then three years later having had no interference from any authorities, something happens to someone else and now everyone's up in arms and wants to make a diagnosis. The day I saw my mother, my teacher of self-respect, my torch, treated like a nobody, doped up to her eyeballs with just enough mental space to think toilet then bed, my sorrows overflowed its cup, there was no hiding place. I began to weep uncontrollably to me, myself and I, rocking from left to right locked in my own embrace as I told my inner child, "There, there girl, don't worry."

Emptiness befell me like no other I had experienced. I felt as if someone had taken an axe to my chest and hacked my heart out. As I watch on paralyzed to the spot my severed flesh collides with the walls, ceilings and floors as spews of my blood, the waterfall of life trickle through the crevices forgotten. My self-belief that love truly existed however slight within humanity had been severely battered and for the first time in my life, I had an enemy. I made a vow to never trust doctors, housing, social services or such alike again. In fact, I vowed never to trust anyone ever.

Tortured by past regrets that rendered me helpless to help my beautiful mother in her time of need who was reduced to a zombie to suffer the moans and groans of other lost souls, I decided going back home wasn't an option anymore, I had to go. If I didn't deal with mother's matters at hand it would escalate into something I could not control. The mere thought of, "What if," the worst happens, and I do nothing to try and stop it was a far greater pain to carry than walking away.

With the understanding that everything is for a reason and that some memories are best forgotten, I convinced myself that this time around things would be different. Deep in my heart I missed my mum and never really left her. I just needed to find my own way in life and discover what lay beyond the realms of mental health. For once I wanted to shine from the inside out and replace my hidden sadness with joy. I thought if I could face my demons against all the odds and survive then maybe, just maybe mum could too.

When I moved back the first thing that became apparent to me was the extensiveness of disrepair to the house. It was in a worse state than I had remembered. The pigeons had taken residence in the attic and half the roof was missing. The bathroom, well that was non-operational, it was the old fashion bucket and water to wash and to flush. The ceilings were decaying creating holes where we could capture streams of rain and the fact there was no heating or electricity, well it didn't help matters. Yep, there's no place like home, "And ain't that the truth."

Whilst things seemed relatively calm for a few weeks I knew mum's elation of, "I'm not alone anymore," would fade away and the, "Norm," would resume itself. It would be a matter of when mother had one of her moments. So, when my cursing eventually came, I took it with half-cocked ears and hardened my heart with a special brew and a spliff. I knew this wasn't the right way forward, but I didn't have the spiritual strength to fight the self. With all the want in my world to be the rescuer, I found myself once again disconnecting from the real world unable to cope with the feelings and faith it demanded.

I was burning out and needed a distraction, I needed to go back to work. Entrenched in a defiant spirit that was determined to break free from labels and sweet F.A. I found work temping as a shop floor assistant at Cullen's in Victoria. I had made some unusual friends to say the least whose visions of life seem to dwell on uncertainty. Little by little I spent more time with them turning the hours into days at a time. Once again, I was experiencing something new in my life, something very different to my own and it intrigued me.

Stepping Out

Just turned seventeen and a quarter, I found work temping in a delicatessen. I worked with a small group of people who were all strange in their own way, yet I found myself drawn to want to be in their company in particular, a man called Mathew. Through him I was introduced into the world of homelessness and found myself enjoying it.

There was something to be said dossing in train carriages only to be moved on by the police or spinning a line to a hotel manager to get a room for the night. As grimy as it was washing in the public toilets early in the morning with barely enough change to get a cup of tea, it seemed to be better than being anywhere else. For the first time I was responsible for only me. I was living a life my school friends could never imagine.

I met so many people from varied backgrounds. Some were accountants and lawyers bummed out through drink and drugs. Some had homes that I'd only ever seen in magazines, yet they preferred the streets and then there were the, "Others," who were just best avoided. From the wanna be entrepreneurs to the guy with the clubfoot, everyone had a story to tell which generally came out in their behavior. It was a strange relationship because the only person you really looked out for was yourself, yet in this group of misfits I felt connected. Connected to the unspoken word that we're all running away from something and you know what, it's okay you're not judged here.

Mathew was a blond hair blue-eyed white man who was twice my age, he was also my first sexual partner. It was the first time that I had dated a white man. I played at not being bothered by this and sung aloud tune of, what should matter is love and not the colour of your skin, yet I had no intention of introducing him to any of my people let alone letting him know where I lived. I'm not sure why I took that stance, maybe something deep down was telling me that the relationship was wrong.

The most Mathew got from me was my grandparents phone number. I was so caught up in me there was no space for Mathew in my heart or mind really. I was looking for a way out from my life dynamics and he seemed to present that ticket. He didn't seem to care for rules or for boundaries, he was messed up even more so than I was.

Mathew was an ex-army guy who spent hard time in prison for pushing his best friend out of a high-rise block of flats, killing him. He lost everything, his liberty, career, women and child. He said it was an accident, but I had seen a jealous streak in him that would easily turn on his brethren for looking at me in the wrong way. He liked a good punch up, to coin a phrase, which might have had something to do with the fact he was short. He always had something to prove. Most of the time I found him quite irritating.

There he was a grown man stacking shelves and hanging out with the homeless crew, "Yeah, you're really going somewhere." It's funny how the very things that once sweet you can leave a sour taste in your mouth. Often, I'd occupy myself with things that put a distance between us. I flipped him like a light switch with no regards to his feelings. I felt burdened by the extra responsibility of having to show care and concern for someone else, whose life's tragedy seemed to be of their own making. What's more, I didn't know how to have a real relationship because I didn't have one with myself. I just wanted someone to be there for me as and when I needed, but not give anything in return. For a while that arrangement worked until my folks found out about him.

By sheer bad luck Mathew calls my grandparents in search of me as I had gone missing for about a week or so. When they realized I was actually having sex, it was a blow. When they realized I was not only having sex, I was having sex with a thirty something year old man it was an even bigger blow. But when they realized, I was having sex with a thirty something year old man who was white, I subconsciously unleashed the hounds. He got a cussing of his life, they called him everything from sunrise to sunset. My dad wasn't best pleased, especially him being a Rastafarian.

It was strange to think that in the past I had spent so much time trying to get the attention of my family to no real satisfaction. Then like a puff of smoke the attention comes, and it saddened me because it wasn't the way I really wanted it. I wanted that raw heart felt passion that stirred up an onslaught on Mathew to be used for something that had genuine purpose in my life like mental health support, not for dating a white man.

If only they could have seen beyond my façade of being with Mathew. My actions had nothing to do with him as selfish as it was. It was all about me wanting and searching for something I thought I had lost. I knew my family's concerns were genuine and if I were sitting on their side of the fence, I would have felt exactly the same way, but I wasn't, and I didn't. I was even more determined to show them that I make the rules for me. So, with my chest held high and my ego super inflated, I maintained my hard girl exterior that had abandoned time for talk and reason and left the wagging tongues wagging with delight.

The moment eventually came when I gave Mathew my virginity. He took me to Hyde Park where the freaks come out at night and almost immediately, I regretted it. I knew he wasn't the one. I made my moments with him a fantasy because that was what I wanted to experience but I wished I had saved it for someone special who I loved and cared for but more importantly, who I believed loved and cared for me.

From then on, I held a deep resentment towards Mathew. I knew in his infinite wisdom of adulthood he took advantage of my troubled young flesh and tainted it with his gunk to fill his lost desires. It left me feeling dirty and frustrated for not taking more care of what was so precious to me. Every time we had sex there after which wasn't very often, I'd purposely tear his back to shreds and make out it was because I couldn't take the pressure.

In the end, I left Mathew literally without warning and to no great loss. In fact, I found the whole experience quite liberating. Something had awoken inside of me one morning that said, "Enough! You don't want this so why are you settling? You too have a life of your own and you can do whatever you want. There's a big world out there just waiting to be explored all you got to do is go for it. No more rocking on the park bench ready to fall. No more waiting for someone to tell me what to do and make it right." It was time for me to come off auto pilot and go into manual drive. I was deciding the pace I wanted to go, I was stepping out.

Fired up by disappointment, I made a split decision to leave home and everyone behind for as long as I could. I told my mum that I was going away for a while and I'd be in touch. I didn't look at her facial expression to my new declaration, neither did I falter to reconsidering. Within five minutes I had packed my world into one bag and headed for Victoria station.

I called my grandparents from the station informing them that I couldn't really talk but that I was going away and then I deliberately cut the phone off. I wanted to cause panic amongst my family, I wanted to see how long it would take them to look for me. My defiance in leaving was a way of demanding the truth by actions. I wanted to be wrong in myself belief that no one truly cared and that all the talk of love was merely that.

I had paired up with a Scottish girl called Kelly who was a homeless veteran and the then girlfriend of Jimmy, who was a friend of Mathews. I persuaded Kelly to come traveling with me and dump Jimmy who was a waste of space who treated her like shit. With nothing to stay for and no reason not to leave, we jumped on a train and decided to go where ever it took us. We were finally kicked off at Hove in the middle of the night. With not a pot to piss in between us, as we hadn't thought that far ahead, I came up with the idea that Kelly should pretend that she's sick, I'd call an ambulance and then we'd crash at the hospital until the morning.

As thought, so done. When we arrived at the hospital, we were left to our own devices in the waiting area. None of the nurses made attempts to move us on, despite the ambulance men reporting that nothing was physically wrong. Neither did anyone ask what two young girls were doing all alone, dead in the middle of the night. I suppose it was a blessing in disguise for if they did where would we have gone. I gave thanks for small mercies and tried to get some sleep.

It sounds so simple, "Getting some sleep," yet it proved virtually impossible for me. I have never sat upon furniture as foreboding as the hospital chair. I tossed and turned continuously and even debated with myself whether sleeping on the streets would be such a bad thing. For as soon as I'd get comfortable, I'd feel a draft that always seemed to find the nape of my neck. It was the bloody air conditioning and it was freezing, I kept thinking if I don't leave here with hypothermia it's a miracle. What's more, every time I looked over at Kelly she seemed to be in a deep and wondrous sleep, how I envied her.

When I awoke the next morning, my back was killing me, I couldn't wait to get out of there and they call it a hospital. I thought, so much for bright ideas but never this one again. I turned to Kelly and said, "Right, first things first, let's find a hostel and the nearest DSS." The system was in its infant stages back then. What you had to do is present a letter from the hostel you were staying at and there and then you'd get an emergency payment over the counter. It was easy. We stayed in various hostels for several weeks, then we moved on to Brighton.

Brighton had a liveliness about it that was very different to Hove. With its bright lights and dazzling peer, it attracted a mixture of shipwrecks both young and old. There was always something to do or somewhere to go. It was a place of opportunity and mystery. At night the streets would take on new form and the beach would come alive once again. I'd often loose myself in its view for hours and allow my mind to drift with the ocean breeze.

Brighton was the breath of fresh air I had craved for even though at times it was like spot the black apart from when the Christian convention came over. I wasn't fearful of the dangers that lay ahead because being black and from Hackney seemed to carry its own weight. I had girls coming up to me asking me to fight their battles just because of where I came from, it was bizarre, but I loved it, I loved the attention. I started to look upon Brighton as a surrogate home, a safe place to retreat that allowed me to be me.

It seems when all the elements are aligned then things can only go right. Within several weeks of settling in Kelly and I befriended a gay couple at the local pub who owned a green grocer. They were oddly matched with their continuous bickering and jibes at one another. One was young and flamboyant and the other old and miserable, yet they were never apart and perfectly matched at being the bitch. The very first night we met them they offered me a job as a sales assistant at their grocery shop, cash in hand.

This boosted my self-esteem, sorted out the drink money and took the edge off the fact we were living in a dump. Our hostel was an old building situated in a square that was by the seashore, well that's the view I got when I turned my head left and looked out of the bedroom window. Our room was small and didn't get much light. The entire house housed at least thirty people. We had to share the bathroom with about twelve other residents on our landing who were all middle age men, not pleasant. The dining area always smelt like old people and seemed covered in a permanent dust that gave an ancient appearance. We never stayed in much. The only compensation was as you left the hostels main door directly in front of it was the front door to the pub.

Come four o'clock I'd get home from work with some groceries where Kelly would always be there to greet me. I'd ask her what she had been doing for the day and she'd always say she'd hung out with the guys from the shelter. We'd have a little munch, I'd change my clothes and then we'd go down to our local pub. We'd stay there for several hours and then we'd take a walk down the beach checking out the local bars and nightclubs. Occasionally Kelly and me would go skinny-dipping and even though the water was freezing, boy did it feel good.

About two months later by chance, we met up with two guys who we had previously met in Hove DSS. Lee a cockney lad and Jimmy the Scotsman, they lived on the next street. Their hostel was modern looking, and all the residents were young and lively. The rooms were spacious and bright, everything looked clean. There was a washing machine and a garden to hang out your clothes. The kitchen and bathroom were shared and there was also a communal room. Not only that, there was enough space for us to have our own rooms. Bish, bash bosh without a second glance we said goodbye to the old hostel and hello to the new.

It was like a carry-on film, every character existed in that hostel from the good guy to the bad guy, from the shady couple to the shady businessman, from the gay guy to the slut, we had it all. It was fun, fun, fun, drama and excitement all at the same time. I had no need for a television I was capturing this shit live. If someone wasn't being arrested or carted off to prison, someone was being hunted down by the mob, if someone wasn't fighting and being disorderly, someone was sleeping with someone they shouldn't. Every so often there'd be a period of calm where the old residents moved out and new one moved in and then before you knew it, dramas would flair up again.

I felt like a bird freed from captivity. I didn't have a real sense of direction I just knew I had to spread my wings and take flight. I seized every moment with no bars held, I wanted to be fed life, so that I could know what it feels like to live. I clean forgot about the life I had left behind. I don't remember speaking about my past throughout my time in Brighton or yet still being asked about it, not even by Kelly. It wasn't necessary to discuss the past for the present told its own story as we travelled through life's busy highway.

As Kelly and I settled in to our new home we started to get better acquainted to Jimmy and Lee. Often all four of us would get together an evening time and have a drink and a laugh. Occasionally Jimmy and I would get intimate. He was meant to be the good time guy, nothing heavy but he'd always tried to make it that little bit more than what it was and it seemed more so when all four of us were together. He'd either do the over touching thing or when mid-flow in a conversation he'd lip-read how sexy I was for all to see and then give a grin that showed how short his teeth were. The looks I used to give him, sheer repulsion. I knew he was only doing it because secretly he knew I secretly liked and wanted Lee and that Lee secretly liked and wanted me.

Jimmy was the insecure type although you wouldn't think it to look at him. He was tall, muscular with plenty dark hair and all the girls fancied him as opposed to Lee, who was short, small build and balding. You would never have believed he was in his mid-twenties. Yet somehow with all of Jimmy's sex appeal and charisma, I couldn't help but feel drawn towards Lee.

I recognized a hurt in him that I had seen in myself, a concoction of failure, disappointment and rejection. He too had come from a place where the want for love had taken a serious bashing. His mask was to act like a big kid always joking around, up for a drink and getting high never staying still for long as though he was afraid of his own shadow. Sex would often cross my mind when I was alone with him, but it was never quite enough to make me go there. It was his companionship, the side of him that was sensitive and gentle that I seemed to seek and want the most.

One day Lee and I went swimming at the local leisure center. We were messing around with one another in the pool getting quite physical when we saw Jimmy looking at us through the glass window with an, "Oh my God," look on his face and then he walked off. We paused for a moment, looked at each other then continued to swim but by then the mood had changed, for we both knew we were guilty in thought. It wasn't long before we went back to the hostel, where we met Kelly and Jimmy. Jimmy had bought some beers in, so we all started drinking. I could tell he was brewing over the swimming pool incident, as he kept dropping little comments here and there about Lee being his long existing friend, but I played oblivious to it.

He later suggested going to a club, but by this time both him and Lee were quite intoxicated, as were Kelly and I. Jimmy acted so stupidly that night, I could barely look at him. It was Lee who was in my mind eye view. When we left the club, we went back to Jimmy's room. With Jimmy sat slumped in a chair totally out of it, Lee starts dropping hints about what he would like to do to me. I'm thinking this could get interesting when out of the blue he stops mid flow in his rambling and with his drunken self begins to undress

Jimmy and put him to bed, carefully tucking him in. That would have been the perfect time to have him on a one to one with no interruptions, but the whole tucking into bed thing threw me off, so I retired to my bed alone.

The next morning slightly soba from the night before, I went looking for Lee to tell him how I really felt only to find out that he had gone. He had packed up and left that night, I was heartbroken. All I had left of him was a pink jumper he had lent me some time ago. I searched for him for days, but I never found him or ever saw him again. Even I know when you don't want to be found, no one is finding you. I was gutted and to boot Jimmy left a week later and went back to Scotland. I hated change where it came without warning as it always left a taste of abandonment in my mouth.

Jimmy and Lee with all their flaws where the one consistent thing in my life for the short time spent in the hostel and when they left it became empty. It would appear from the moment of their departure the whole house seemed to break down. It came out in the wash that the person responsible for collecting the rent from the residence was swindling the landlord out of his money and had gone into hiding because he had, had sex with an underage boy whose family where East End gangsters and they wanted him dead.

Even the relationship between Kelly and I started to drift apart. As time went on, we started spending less and less time together. It became evident that we didn't really have anything in common and I really didn't do hanging out at the shelter. I wanted something more stable and working gave me the freedom to feel like that. I was beginning to think of my room as my place. I started buying things as though building towards a future. I was seriously contemplating setting up permanently in Brighton and that's when thoughts of home started to run through my mind.

There's No Place Like Home

As thoughts of home started to flood my mind, I plucked up the courage and decided I would go back for a visit. I wasn't sure who I was going to see although it was a chance for me to get my black products. I told Kelly I was going to see my family, but I would be back that night. When I arrived in London Victory, I felt animated by stepping upon old grounds. The same grounds I had wanted to bury for so long that was now comforting me. It was like sleeping in my old bed but with new bedding. There was something releasing in being able to go back and retake those first step.

As I headed towards my old haunts to see if I could spot any of the homeless massive, it became apparent that nothing was familiar to me anymore. The area had changed so much. I started to question just how long I had been away for. The only thing that was the same was the café where we would sometimes sit and share a cup of tea. With a sigh I jumped on a 38 bus and headed for lower Clapton to the hair dresses. Once my hair was done, I bought some products and then went straight to see my sister Cecile.

I chose not to see the rest of my family on this occasion because I wasn't sure if I was ever coming back. Besides, I wasn't ready for the questions that would follow. I was still hanging on a string that someone, somewhere would come looking for me. At Cecile's we sat for a few hours' chit chatting about my escapades and the people I had met. We even briefly spoke about mum. I was of the impression she had only seen her in passing during the time I had been away. It troubled me that she was all alone, yet it was not enough to instigate me to go and see her, not then.

So engrossed were Cecile and I in conversation before I could blink twice the clock was saying, "Rap it up now." I felt sad to leave my sister. There was so much I wanted to say. It was refreshing to talk to someone who truly understood me and who would show patience to wade through the many thoughts and feelings that had me knotted up all inside. But it seems there is never enough time in the day when you want it. Whatever I had to say it would have to keep, for time was not permitting. With that I said my goodbyes forward bound to Victory Station to catch the last coach back to Brighton.

On my journey home my heart pined for mum. Talk about a rock and a hard place. I wanted to see her I really did, but I knew at that time I might not find the courage to leave as I once did before. It plagued me not knowing if she was okay and if anyone was looking out for her. I wondered if she was as lonely as I was. When I arrived back in Brighton, I bought myself a beer, some fags and retired to my room alone. I spoke to no one that night, I needed time to lick my wounds and convalesce.

Several weeks had passed before I decided to visit home for the second time. I really wanted to see my sister and walk on familiar turf. It seems like there's no place like home for real, even if it resembles memories of broken biscuits. From the first time I went back, in the midst of my mixed emotions, somehow something was set free inside of me. I didn't feel the same anxieties as before because I knew I could get leave at any time. I had somewhere of my own to go to and I liked the thought of traveling between two homes. I'm glad I took those first steps because it provided me with the remedy I needed, even if I didn't fully understand it at the time.

As before I went to the hairdressers and then to my sisters, avoiding any friends or family members. On the coach journey back to Brighton thoughts of mum churned through my head once again, as I pondered on the familiar routes, I had walked that day. Everywhere told a story of memories past that seemed to clog up my arteries and suffocate my brain. I couldn't breathe for the want of living. With my invisible blanket of woe placed firmly upon my shoulders my heart weighed heavy that night.

The next morning, I awoke refreshed. Somehow from the moment I closed my eyes I arouse to a new dawn. I had decided I was going traveling abroad, somewhere like Spain to start. Whilst this decision would mean further distancing myself from my family, I felt the need to shape my own destiny. It wasn't about running away anymore because all I ever seemed to do is run back into myself. Bravely I clung to, my life is what I choose it to be and it's with a mother who also has mental health. Enough with the trying to forget because all I secretly do is remember. I needed to face things head on and put my demons out of business. For that to happen, for me to set out on my one-man band exploration, I needed to go back home and face mum one more time.

As steadfast as I was in my ambitions to be free, saying goodbye to Brighton wasn't easy. I took my time to savor moments with friends, a place that had become a safe haven to me of which I'll never forget but probably never visit again. Every moment I had to myself I took to the beach and got lost in the seas view, allowing my mind to surf the waves and think beyond the horizon. Then one morning something said, "It's time to prepare to leave."

I handed in my notice at the grocery store that day and went on a three-day beer binge with Kelly. We never spoke of seeing each other again or keeping in touch, we just drunk beer and laughed the moment away like when we first met. That was another one of those unspoken rules, no one ever said goodbye.

Upon the fourth day, a Saturday I awoke to the sun shining bright. I was packed from the night before and good to go. Kelly and I walked to the coach depot in a reminiscent silence. I kept looking at her and she too at me, but we never said anything apart from smile at on another. I knew I was going to miss her, and I had the feeling that she too was going to miss me. We had come to an end of an era Kelly and I. The same elements that had caused our paths to cross, were the very same things that would now separate us. Yet somehow this time around, it didn't feel wrong or like I was losing something, for within I had gained so much from the time we had shared. Lessons of learning and memories I could never forget, I had grown.

As I boarded the coach and took my seat our smiles grew larger and we began waving at each other overly excited until the coach pulled away. My face felt like it had been stretched apart and my jaw ached. When I could no longer see her smiley face or waving hand, I rested my head upon the window and photographed the last pieces of scenery with my eyes.

Why does the journey going home always feel shorter than the journey leaving? As quick as I had left home was as quick as I found myself standing back at the foot of my front door. It felt as if I had popped to the shops and was now returning home. It was a curious feeling. For a while I stood starring at my bedroom window feeling for signs of presence. It was still there, but it wasn't as strong as it once was. Maybe it knew I had come home to vanquish it. With a sigh of, "It's now or never," I put on my brave face and went and knocked on the door.

"Mummy," I called through the letterbox as I flickered my eyelids to see signs of life. I hadn't called her that for what seems like forever and yet it came so naturally to me. "Mummy," I called again completing forgetting she only responded to the name Pauline. I heard a shuffling and then the sound of footsteps drawing closer to me. Within seconds mum had come downstairs and opened the door, an all-time best I'm sure. She's never opened the door as quick as that before. It was a good sign.

I had rehearsed this moment in my head several times over. I was going to say, "You alright mum? How you doing? Look, I'm going away for a while and I'm not sure when I'll be back but is it all right if I stay for a few days." But when I saw her little face with the expression of elatedness and disbelief as though questioning, "Is it really you?" I couldn't break her heart so all I said was, "You alright mum?" There was a brief pause and then she nodded her head. With this I walked upstairs and put my bags down in her old room to the back of the house.

It was strange to see that so much of the environment had changed around me, yet home remained exactly the same. Whilst I felt a sense of relief being home my anxieties kept telling me, "Don't get to comfortable you're not stopping for long." I didn't want to lose that get up and go in me. Living independently placed my destiny in my own hands. Upon a blank canvass I could create the path in which I wanted to go. For the first time I understood how you manage life. A burning question I always thought of as a small child to which the answer is, you live.

When I came down stairs into the sitting room where mother was sat on the sofa. I sat on some boxes that she meticulously placed in the center of the room. The atmosphere was calm as rays of light shone through the windows warming up the room. For a while mother and I just sat looking at each other. I could see that, "I missed you," look in her eyes. She looked extremely well for someone I worried so much about, God only knows how she was surviving, but she was. I missed her so much, but I wasn't sure how to let the words flow, so I said, "So how have you been?"

"Oh, I'm okay," she replied in a childlike manner. "So," I continued, "So what have you been doing with yourself?" She began to rub her hands between her legs and pulled a baby type face and said, "Just working hard you know." The only time I had seen my mum looking so vulnerable was just before her major nervous breakdown. I could see in her display of innocence she was saying, "I need you, don't leave me Shavon." I wanted to hold her so much, but I was scared. The last time I remember my mother embracing me was when I was thirteen years old. I'm now eighteen and a half, I couldn't be sure she wouldn't reject me, and I hadn't prepared for that, so I tried to comfort her with my eyes.

She asked me how I had been which I always replied, "I'm alright." But the more I looked at her the more over whelmed I became with, "I wish, I wish my mum were back to normal." My heart was going into melt down and I thought my plans of Jackanory would most certainly be over. Holding back the tears I hastened my thoughts together and told mum that I had saved some money. I placed eighty quid on the side and said that I was going out for a while. I was going to see Cecile and I'd be back later.

I didn't have to go far as Cecile was at a birthday celebration at her daughter's dads, mum's house, which was only around the corner from mums. Everyone seemed happy to see me as if they knew I had been missing. "Come take a brandy," said Miss Hope as she handed me a glass with a spliff packed with weed. I knew that mixing spirits after a three-day beer binge would not end well but, resistance was futile. With a couple of sips and several pulls, I started to feel woozy and very hot, I needed air.

On the verge of collapsing but not wanting to look like a total looser, I managed to compose myself until I reached the outside and not before time too. As soon as the fresh air hit my face I began to pour with sweat, passersby kept looking at me funny. Conscious I only had a matter of minutes before my legs gave way on me, I headed to the nearest front garden and lay on the floor quietly hoping I'd cool down, the buzz would ware off, the world would stop spinning and no one would see me.

In the distance which was literally across the road, I could hear my sister calling my name, "Shavon, Shavon," pausing for a moment and then saying, "Maybe she's gone home." I dear not answer for the shame of it but let the truth be known I couldn't answer. I wasn't in control of my

113

speech, I wasn't in control of anything. I was totally wasted.

The next morning, I woke up at home perfectly incased in my sleeping bag, snug as a rug as they say. I even had my nightclothes on. As I let my eyes drift around the room, I saw the money I had given mum the day before beside me. I kept thinking when, how and who took me home? All I could remember was feeling on fire and trying to cool myself down in someone's front garden. The rest of the night was a total blank to me yet somehow, I felt rejuvenated. I was sure I'd be reminded at some point during the day how and who had to carry me home, but no one ever did come forward.

I decided it was time to see the rest of my family. It was time to bridge the gap. I freshened up, old time style-lee, bucket and cold water and went to see my grandparents around dinnertime. When my gran saw me, she nearly fainted. The first thing she said was, "Are you pregnant?" to which I replied a flat, "No grandmother." Yvonne and Sybil just stood in amazement. "Your back then," said Yvonne in Yvonne's way. I smiled. "You alright Shivs," said Sybil to which I nodded. My granddad acted neither surprised nor perturbed by my presence. I gave him a kiss as I always do and said, "You alright granddad," to which he replied, "Yes," in his Jamaican way.

The atmosphere at my grans was theatrical yet perfectly functional. I started to see that some things just, are. That afternoon I tucked into some good old Jamaican food until my belly buss. Again, a hurdle had been jumped and a small victory had been won. I had taken a leap of faith and was reunited with my family that left me smiling. Whilst I knew that things would never be the same, I welcomed the change for I was learning fast that real change starts within yourself.

About two weeks later mum started to ask me for money. I didn't think anything of it at first until the third week. I noticed she hadn't gone to sign on at any time. With further investigation I discovered mother had stopped signing on months ago and her housing benefit had been cancelled. Here we go again, even if I wanted to go I couldn't now, not until I sorted out this mess, which could take months.

Resigning myself to, "I won't be leaving anytime soon," I flung my notion of, "I only came back to say goodbye," out the window. Ironically it would seem by virtue that where I needed to be was where I ended up and all in perfect timing. I became mother's guardian with the responsibility of the maintenance of her finances. I stopped believing in coincidences that day and started to listen more to the inner voices, the visions, the dreams that guided me through life's ups and downs, warning me of things to come and directions I needed to go.

The universe with its divinity has always played its part in my life from every moment of joy to every disappointment. Many times, I have placed my cries and prayers upon the Fathers alter and the message has been received and an answer sent. I needed no more confirmation on where I needed to be or what I had to do. I had gone all around the houses only to run back into myself, exactly the same point from which I left. What I could not see before now seemed so clear, my eyes were beginning to open, and I felt enriched with foresight.

Learning that the double edge sword of living to forget, was nothing more than forgetting to live. I was of the realization that it was no longer, Why me? It was, Why not me? Would I really wish my burden upon someone else to carry? And if so, who would that someone else be?

With all my intricacies and imperfections, I was discovering I could walk for the first time, just like a child discovering they have legs. My mind was being strengthened, my spirit filled, and my physical being matured. I was being prepared for the struggles I had subconsciously chosen to fight but this time my armor was understanding and my shield faith. Anger was beginning to lose the war it had waged against me even though, I knew there were plenty more battles still to fight.

Mother's home situation was, "Functioning," on an even keel, let us just say that. But I knew I couldn't watch over her twenty-four seven and at some point in time, outside agencies would get involved in her life once again, not because she needed help but because the house was falling apart. I knew being back home would mean walking past steps and crying old tears but that didn't bother me, for I knew it was for a higher purpose.

For hours mum and I would sit and talk all sorts of nonsense yet still there was sense to be picked. Mum had a knack of portraying herself as, "Not all the ticket," but there was more method to her madness than you'd think, especially if she was looking a little change. We'd eat chicken and chips, have a smoke, drink two liquor and buss a few jokes. We laughed together like mother and daughter. Often, I'd found myself gazing at her face full of tears in my heart. I missed her, I missed **MY MUM**.

I could only wonder what things would have been like if our circumstances where different. Cecile reckons mum would have been living in another country, probably Jamaica, she always talked about wanting to go home but adamant she' not getting on an airplane, "Who me?" she'd always say. One thing I do know, wherever mum would have ended up, I wouldn't be far away. I don't think my heart could endure a peaceful sleep if I couldn't be sure that she was all right. I was glad to be home.

As I settled in to a routine of being, I re-established some of my old friendships telling all who'd want to listen of my adventures. It was just like old times, it was as if I hadn't been away. Chanika and the gang were just as funny as ever all blooming into adulthood. Taneil still lived at the hostel with Corrie and the other guys. They all said I should write a book little did they know I wanted to too. "One day, one day."

I even found some receptionist work in a clothes warehouse. The money wasn't great, and the people were rude, but it was better than nothing. It felt good to be able to make my own decisions, reaffirm old relationships and make new ones. The doctor couldn't have ordered a better pill to replace the loss of Brighton. I was having fun and enjoying rebuilding my life. I felt like I was on top again.

I levitated to spending more time at Taneil's place. The hostel was the meeting ground for all the man's dem, everybody passed through. I fitted in like a glove, as I was more the tomboy type. The guys viewed me as one of them, sometimes we'd all go raving together. Secretly I wallowed in their excitement, attention and testosterone. Even Taneil and I seemed to get closer, it was all good. Whatever rejuvenation was taking place in my life, it was doing a full three-hundred-and-sixty-degree turn.

In The Namesake Of Love

Taneil was a dark skinned, gold tooth, fit black brother. I always fancied the socks off him, but because we lived in the same hostel and we were such good friends I thought it better not to go there. However, that was back then. Sometimes he'd come over as the quiet type, but when he was on a role, he was the life and sole of any party.

As our friendship blossomed, we began to share deeper experiences of our lives with each other. I learned that he too had come from a similar place of odd goings on where the mere mention of, "Mother," resonated complex issues. At one point we even thought we might had been related. As a small child I knew his grandmother who I always thought was related to my mum because we were always playing at her sewing shop based in Church Street. Could it be Taneil and I have crossed paths once before as children? Now what are the odds on that?

Armored like two peas in a pod our friendship progressed to a relationship. We often spoke of dreams and aspirations where we were the captains of the ship. No matter how far away or farfetched those aspirations sounded, I could always close my eyes and visualize what it would look like in its completeness, kicking back in splendor, whilst looking on with satisfaction at what our hard work and perseverance had achieved. It was all that, "One man's determination can inspire a nation to do great things they never thought possible," talk. Dreams to me were things that could come true if you really wanted it and boy, I wanted it.

Six months later we were planning our lives around a baby soon to come. When I plucked up the courage to tell mum she ended my sentence for me with, "Your pregnant," she already knew. She said she was a bit disappointed, but it was my choice. I didn't have the heart to tell her that we had planned it and that at some point I would need to move out because the house wasn't safe to raise a baby. I remember her being calm and composed in her understanding. I almost got the impression by her body language that she was saying, "There's no turning back now, you're going to see now."

It was strange to think of mum being a grandmother as she never played an active part in Shantel's life, so I had no way of knowing how she would adapt to my circumstances. I wanted her to be beside me on my new journey, but I knew for the relationship it would mean less time for her. Call it inevitable change or destiny, but mother would now be challenged to re-engage in some of those independent skills she once possessed, and I had no choice but to let go of some of mines.

What an expedition of self this has become for in my fear sate of rejection, disappointment and distrust, I carried the world upon my shoulders and allowed nobody in. I had spoilt mum to only rely upon me by trying to be the, "Everything," even though it nearly half killed me. In doing so she accepted no one else but me. However, with new responsibilities to consider beyond myself, I was beginning to see the rod I'd been making off my own back. Finally, my old way of being would have to change.

Pleasantly over the months of my pregnancy mother and I began to bond differently. We were having mother and daughter moments of laughter and reminiscing. She showered me with attention and was attentive to my every need always asking if I had eaten or if I was hungry. I loved the way we were growing and experiencing normality together, fusing just right like cake and custard.

It sounds surreal, but it was like a wildlife scene where the mother raises her young into adults, teaching them all they need to know on how to survive and then sending them out into the world to find a new location and lay their own foundations to call home. Everything was as it should be.

Taneil and I started making all sorts of plans. We were going to elope and have a low-key wedding and when we could afford a proper do, we'd announce it to our families that we were getting married as not to be seen to be breaking tradition. Together we were carving templates of our existence to last a lifetime and then some.

The first time he told me he loved me it moved me to tears. At that time in my life I didn't whole heartedly believe that I possessed anything great that someone would want to love yet here was this man looking into my eyes with a genuineness that pierced the very core of my heart whispering words I'd been longing to hear, "I love you."

So drunk in love was I for Taneil, I placed him upon

a pedestal that had him sat amongst the clouds where the expectations were high and the future ambitious. I was determined to manifest the home I felt denied with a leader strong in his entirety by my side. I would be his spine and he my rock. The shoes to be filled were huge and in it I had placed my all.

For a while, things ran fairly smoothly between us, but as the pregnancy took a hold of my body my entire emotions took a hold of me. One minute I was up and then the next I was down. I would have bursts of energy where I felt I could run a marathon or go ten rounds in a boxing ring all accompanied by explosions of tears filled with woe. I was a nightmare. Taneil tried hard to cope with my sporadic outbursts but his tolerance would sometimes give way and he'd show a cold side of him that left me literally freezing.

Eight months later I broke the news to mum that I had to move out and make preparations for the baby. I didn't want to leave her, but I couldn't stay in the house. She took it well and made no fuss. I knew she'd feel lonely for a while, but it wouldn't be for long and I wouldn't be too far away. Later that month Taneil was placed in a semi-independent living hostel down Stamford Hill and I moved in with him.

I've now reached full term of my pregnancy when I turned to Taneil one morning and said, "I'm sure the baby due today, shouldn't we go down the hospital?" He agreed and off we set. When we arrived, I went to the receptionist and said, "Excuse me, I'm sure my baby is due today but nothings really happening, so we thought we'd come down and check it out." They were concerned that they didn't have many notes on me, that's when I explained I never knew I had to have checkups, I thought you just go to the doctor they confirm your pregnant, they give you a due date and when it's time you turn up at the hospital, have your child and that's you.

Needless to say, they kept me in and induced me as there wasn't a lot of fluid around the baby and I hadn't dilated. Taneil did his best to reassure me but after the twenty-third hour of labour pains it really didn't matter if he was in the room or not. To boot the midwife who examined me looked like a black version of the, "She Devil," she even had a mole on the side of her face.

With a stance of iron and a push up mouth that read, "Show no mercy," she thrusts her fingers up inside me. I'm not sure what she was searching for but it sure weren't for a baby. Instantaneously tears filled my eyes and began to flood my face. Effortlessly she was making my experience of childbirth a living hell. Not a soft word did she utter in fact, she didn't speak at all apart from ordering me to open my legs. I felt she was punishing me for being young, black and pregnant but my dramas never ended there.

Twenty-four hours later I'm now in the delivery suite legs sprawled apart for all in sundry to see, screaming my head off like a mother foe, panting on the verge of passing out because I never went antenatal classes and learnt how to breath. All of a sudden, a nurse enters the room, takes my hand and begins to stroke it. She spoke with words of kindness that sounded so angelic. I started to relax and feel safe. However, that moment was short lived when she asked, "Do you mind if some students come in and observe you giving birth?"

Psychologically and physiologically I was still a bit dazed by the whole labour thing, but I was definitely coherent enough with eyes opened wide to tell her a firm, "No." All of a sudden, I hear a thump on the bed. I looked down to see what had made the noise, it was then that I realized it was indeed my own hand. She had let go with such speed I wasn't even aware she had done it. The last glimpse of her I saw was her back as she left the room and still there was more to come.

In total astonishment that a nurse had just duped me, my next contraction came, and I went into panic mode. I couldn't push when I should and pushed when I shouldn't, I was exhausted from being exhausted. The Midwives decided the best chance to get baby out was to cut me. I couldn't feel a thing but as I looked on, instead of the scissors cutting a straight line it just twisted up my skin. The scissors were blunt. Needless to say, several attempts were made before success came.

I began to reflect as I lay with my legs in stirrups and the baby's head at the tip of my virgina. First, I was manhandled by the, "She Devil," then I was manipulated by a, "Duping nurse," and then I was surgically incised with scissors that didn't want to cut. If the words could have transcended from my mouth, what a story I would have told them however, all I wanted, was to get out of there. So, with all the strength I could muster I gave an almighty push and that's when my little baby girl popped into the world.

As soon as she came out, my stomach deflated instantly. I know it sounds strange because we all know about the birds and the bee's but, I was in shock to see this little person come out from inside of me. She was perfect in her design, she was beautiful. I looked on in wonder, as I was too shattered to hold her straightaway. It was a nurse who dressed her and laid her in a cot covering her with a blanket. I kept looking at her for about five minutes thinking, I wonder if she has enough air to breath. I then leaned over and pulled back the blanket slightly. That was the sealing moment of my love for my beautiful big brown eyes baby. So, I wrote her a letter.

My sweet Munroe, you're chubby and cry mainly when you're hungry. You have a beautiful smile, and everybody adores you, I love you so much and have no doubt in my mind that you are the best thing that could have ever happened to me.

Every day I see you, I fall in love with you more. I just want to squeeze and transfer all my love into you. There's so much that I am going to learn from you and so much you are going to learn from me. I'm going to teach you manners, respect for others, to love and be kind. I will teach you the difference between right and wrong. I want you to be able to tell me anything if ever you have a problem. I don't want you to be scared of me, I want you to trust me as I have put my trust in you.

I'll never stop loving you and will always be by your side. I will try and help and understand you to the best of my abilities by being a mother you can be proud of, so you can hold you head up high and say to all your friends, "That's my mum," I love you, mum.

I now sat upon the other side of the fence as the caretaker, the soft place to fall. I had brought a child into this world that at some point in her life would question loving me, just like I had questioned loving mummy. What stories would she tell of me? What lessons would she have learnt? I was going to have to face the highs and lows of seeing my child grow into an adult, modeled on my template of life choices. Could I do better where others had not? Did I even know what I was doing? Had I thoroughly thought everything through? Probably not.

By the end of the first month of Munroe's birth, tragedy had struck once again turning my world upside down. Nicky had been fatally shot in a night club. He passed away before I reached the hospital, but I refused to believe it until I saw his face. I thought no matter what injury he had received, he would wake up for me. My presence and energy would heal and restore him back to me, he would be the living miracle that not even the top scientist could explain. I believed in our spiritual connection, I believed he would awake for me.

When I entered the emergency room, my breathe was taken away. In this room there were other people waiting to die. I was surrounded by death. I shrieked his name, "Nicky," he never replied. My legs became weak and for a moment my mind went blank and when I came to, I was leaning against a wall. For a few seconds I stood afar watching him. He lay perfectly still on the hospital bed, covered with a white sheet from the chest down, yet still in my mind I needed to look into his eyes, I needed to see, I needed to know if he would awake for me.

As I drew near, I found myself by his side, his eyes were slightly open, he sometimes slept like that. I know it makes no sense but for a brief moment I felt hope. I searched deep within his eyes to find that spark, that light that had protected me for so long, my sword, my shield, a true solider on the battle field with the spirit of many warriors of hearts. I called upon the universe to give me strength to make him arise, but he did not steer neither did I find that bright light I was searching for. As silent tears rolled down my face, I leaned in to kiss him for the very last time. As I did so, I was literally thrown back at how cold he felt. That touch of coldness shot me back into reality cementing my hopes and fears all into one. Life had departed, he was gone and with all the best will in the world, he was never coming back.

These people who took his life couldn't really have known the consequences they had unleashed unto themselves for slaying one of the Most High children, for slaying my brother. If they truly did, they would never have done it. In taking of his life they had destroyed a far greater number. I don't fear many things, but I do the wroth of the Almighty. They perpetrated the worse kind of act of desecration against their own to appease their perverse minds and disease-ridden spirits. Everybody's so much in love in trying to get into a coffin, thirsty to drink from the half empty cup of abomination, selling their souls foolishly for illusionary riches, only to find in the end, in their last breath, last thought, last feeling, last word, last day, none of it was gold.

Not only had I lost my beloved brother, I was left with the job of telling my mother. Had she not suffered enough? When Nicky was about seven or eight years old, a group of us were playing out on the streets in front of the flats. We were trying to sell empty lemonade bottles and doing penny for the guy when out of nowhere he's knocked over by a car, some Jewish guy was driving. I ran straight to my mum to let her know and her first response was to slap me in the face, shock, I guess. How was she going to react now? How was I going to tell her that her champion wasn't just hurt but that he was now dead?

As felt within my spirit, when that moment of walking in my truth and standing in my pain came, mother struck out once again but this time her hand did not connect. I knew she understood from her reaction. Grieving with her was abstract. I told her about the funeral and where it would be, but I knew she wouldn't be accompanying me. I just knew.

To my surprise on the day of Nicky funeral just as we were making the walk with the coffin from the church back to the hearse, I saw mum walk pass with a friend. She didn't stop but I know she saw the coffin. Maybe that was Nicky's way of saying goodbye to her himself. Intentionally or unintentionally seeing mum that day offered me some comfort for, for a few seconds my family was all together again.

Is it coincidence that the week before Nicky died I saw him on the road? We stopped and chatted for a while about how he was feeling. He was going through many transformations at that time. He was trying to live a more humble, spiritual fulfilled life, he had withdrawn from the road life mentality and studying accounting, but he was always weighted down with the struggles like most young black men of his time, that lack of mentality, lack of materialism. He said to me, "Shavon, I can't do it man, it's hard man. I don't have money, clothes. I'm struggling right about now. I want to go to Amsterdam for a week to get away for a bit." I knew what that meant. I urged him, "Look towards the future and the rewards you know you stand to gain Nick, they are far greater than anything material you're seeking right now. You can't throw the covering of the Father away for material gain, you know how this thing works," he replied, "I know, I know." I know he heard me but unfortunately, he never paid heed to my words.

Later that afternoon I saw him once again but this time he was across the road. I'm not sure why but I couldn't signal to him to see me, I even tried to call his name but as I opened my mouth it was if something held my throat, so no sound or words would flow. As I sat in the seat of observer, I could see he had on new clothes. A new black Leather

126

jacket, trainers, jeans, fat gold chaps on either wrist. Yes, indeed he looked like he was on top of his game, I could see that in his stride. That is when I knew he had made his decision and he had stepped back to his old ways.

The last time we spoke he had just come back from Amsterdam. He was glowing, full of life and as always, looking slick. He told me how much fun he had, had and that he was definitely going back. I could see the child in him who had just been given a new toy they have always wanted however, the traces of the man I knew who would scatter water over everybody and everything as he said his morning prayers of thanks and protection was gone. He had put that side of being, thinking, feeling to one side, he had turned his back on the very thing that was protecting him and in doing so, he evoked old behaviors, old mind sets, old desires, revisiting old haunts thus resurrecting old problems.

A contract requires two actions, an offer and agreement and when it's broken or dishonored, recompense is required. It was only after his death that I was able to put the pieces together for I had dreamt his death some several years prior and I remember questioning him who he had he troubled for they were known North, South, East and West. I saw him in a car with a group of friends driving into the heart of what seemed like a riot but only his face looked ashy and I knew he was dead. He did not tell me the trouble he had found himself in which were linked to his friends never the less, he was forewarned from me about his life choices, decisions and consequences. That was the second time I had dreamt death in the family, and I was going to be sure this time, I passed on the message.

We spoke for hours as I interpreted what I saw, and it must have had a deeper impact upon him for, for a while he was turning his life around, he had relinquished himself from the environment, mindset and life style that was detrimental to him. But ultimately, in the end he slipped back into cognitive dissonance in the wanting of things. A moment's thought to appease the ego had led him to his death.

I was disheartened with him for some time for making those life choices likewise, I also carried the guilt of, could I have said something more that would have made him change his mind. It left me feeling empty and searching for answers for what seemed like an eternity. If I saw anyone who vaguely resembled him, I would go out of my way to see their faces just to be sure. I clung to a glimmer of hope that maybe what I saw in hospital that day was not my brother and the whole thing was just a massive mistake or bad dream. Needless to say, I always walked away dejected. A void came over me like no other, I felt defenseless without his guidance or protection.

During this time Cecile and I relationship started to drift apart on rapid. I hoped that Nicky's death would have brought us closer together, but it only seemed to do the opposite. She was delving deeper into drugs than before and spiraling out of control, she was even high at his funeral. I pretended I didn't see it, but I saw it all. I had lost my brother and now I was about to lose my sister. Arguments flared up between us and the wider family over some of my brothers' things. I didn't have the strength to fight anymore and began to withdraw, that's when Nicky came to me in a vision twice.

The first time was not long after he had passed away. He had come to my grans house, all the siblings were sitting outside, and I asked him, "What are you doing here? he didn't seem to understand and then I said, "Your dead." He was so angry when I said that, that he stormed off, I was concerned that I might not see him again. The second time he came to me at my sisters flat, this was during the time of the arguments amongst my family regarding his things. We spoke about it and I expressed my sadness and the feelings of being torn apart by it. I told him it meant nothing to me if he wasn't profiling it. He reassured me that it didn't mean anything to him, it was just material things and not to worry about it. He always did know the right thing to say to me and it was exactly what I felt and what I needed to hear. When I awoke from that sleep all my worries regarding my family and my brothers' things had been lifted. If it meant nothing to him, then it meant nothing to me and that I made known to my family, I was done.

For the first few months I was just costing through when I received word that Cecile had fallen out of her bedroom window, three stories high and was now in hospital. Miraculously no bones were broken however, she did slightly damage one of her eyes, but she retained her full sight. If it was not for the fact, she was drunk and that she fell onto a mound and then rolled to the ground as opposed to a straight fall, her ending might have been a lot different. All I could think of was, I was not prepared to bury my sister. From then on whatever discord I felt towards my sister I quashed it in my heart and mind. I had lost enough and wanted to make amends.

I've known of many who live with the regret, remorse, and endless pain for the harsh last words they exchanged with a loved one passed away. Never being able to take it back or say how you truly felt or even correct it. I didn't want this to be me. I didn't want to carry guilt of words of the heart unsaid. Conscious can really be a killer.

I chose to accept Cecile for the person she had chosen to be along with the life choices she made even if it led her to her death. In the past I spent years fighting and cursing at my sister, believing it was my responsibility to get her to change according to me. By carrying her burden of life choices, I restricted the relationship from growing within me. In this life changing moment, I found an acceptance that allowed me to embrace my sister and show her love. By doing this I gave myself permission to be her sister once again.

From there on, our relationship became solid in a way that was healthy for us both. The days of the catfights and unforgiving words had long since been buried and now we stood upon a new ground of sisterhood. A new foundation of togetherness that once formed has never been broken.

A year or so later my relationship with Taneil broke down. I started to look at life differently, focusing more on the spiritual side of my being, honoring that inner voice. When I think back, a lot of what myself and Taneil had in common was our chronicles of sadness but as that veil of desensitization began to raise, it became evident to me we were miles apart in our similarities and even further away in our passions. We put on a good front of being a happy couple but behind the scenes there were plenty tears, disappointment and fighting and in the middle of it all, was an innocent child.

The last thing I ever wanted was to have a family and not be with the father, family meant everything to me however, I knew only too well the ripple effects on the human spirit when we hold on and turn a blind eye to what you know is wrong. I thought hard about the path I wanted to take and the message it would imprint upon my daughters developing mind, as well as the lasting impact it would have upon her later down in life. Taneil was my first love but, my child's happiness, for now and the future is my forever love. I walked away from the relationship.

Whilst I felt a sense of emotional and mentally relief, the spiritual liberation of walking in my truth wasn't an easy path to cross. For as soon as I stepped over that line, stepped into my own space, became the wheel turner in the relationship of me, Taneils presence and input started to fade into the background to the brink of obscurity. In my eyes, just as his father had done unto him, as mine had done unto me, he had done unto his own child, a feeling we both knew only too well. That was the hardest weight to carry, for no amount of love would ease that feeling she would carry throughout her life until she could make sense of it, regarding the lack of interaction and intervention from her father. It was a devastating blow from a dream constructed in heaven, never the less, it was a cross I was prepared to take up and bare.

For the next year or so I stayed at various mother and baby hostels. There were many trials and tribulations to establish my new self, raise a child and build a home, at times life seemed unbearable. One day I decided to take myself to the doctors for a general checkup well, it's primarily because one day my sister said to me, "I could pass for a crack head." Weighing in at a measly seven and a half stone the doctors rudely awoke me to, if I lost any more weight, I could develop an eating disorder.

Clearly life was taking its toll on my physicality and mother could sense that too. What would I have done without her? She may have been diagnosed as a chronic schizophrenic with a thought pattern disorder, but she was one of the most genteel, smart and loving woman, I knew. She always encouraged me to eat and to go out even if it was just for a walk. Perhaps she could see the same depression brewing in me that she once felt within herself. Throughout Munroe's early years her support was un measurable, she allowed me the freedom of being youthful. Sometimes I took the piss, but I was always internally grateful.

Eventually I was offered a massive two-bedroom house just up the road from mums which helped to cement the bond between us. Occasionally mum would stay over on babysitting duties, she even had a boyfriend for a short while, the same guy Nicky flipped over several years prior, putting a knife to his throat warning him, if he made a wrong move against mummy or me, he would kill him. The guy wasn't so bad, he didn't say more than, "Hello," and "Goodbye," which was more than what he said when I first met him, but he was pleasant enough. Mum had things to do, places to go and people to see, her whole persona was changing. She was engaging in living through choice. Often, she would come baring gifts, we'd cook and eat as a family, watch TV, listen to music and laugh, dance and prance.

Pauline rarely serviced to assault me with her words of profanity and when she did, it always came with low level ramblings at which point I would ask her, "Who are you talking to?" to break her trail of thought. She would just stop mid flow and go back to, quote and unquote, "Our normal." We had established a new routine and it was working better than I could have imagined. The issue of mother's house wasn't going to go away no matter which way I looked at it, but I decided I'd cross that bridge when I had to.

The Women In Me

Being a single mother with the pressure to provide was constant. How mum managed three children I will never know. It's the hardest, most time and energy consuming job I have ever signed up for. There were times when I would break down and cry in total despair, "Father help me," but then there were times in the midst of my chaotic moments, I would see rewards given that were priceless like, the first solo part my daughter had in her school play or that first card she made that said, I love you mum. Knowing all of what I had experienced and all that she was experiencing my baby girl was turning out fine.

I occupied my mind with temping here and there whilst studying in the evenings, I was determined to give myself the opportunity to raise my own consciousness to attain my heart desires and aspirations. I knew there was a world out there that offered more, and I wanted a piece of it, but I had to prepare. I held my corner and took care of what was mine, but behind the daily mask something was missing for me, it was male companionship. I tended to form more male friendship than I did with females, I felt comfortable in their presence and environment, I learnt stuff.

Deep down I was looking for a figure that could defend me like my brother, that somebody I could be open with, be myself, share my truths and my shame. There'd be no need for airs and graces for they intrinsically would understand my indifferences yet love me regardless. I wanted a formidable solider on the battle field that reflected the solider within me. I wanted somebody solid yet gentle enough to catch my tears and make me smile, to know within him I have a spine and for him to be wise enough to steer me right when I go wrong yet never waiver in his loyalty. You might think what a romanticized notion of a fictious person, but that was my brother. He had raised the bar high for me so, without consciously thinking it, I was trying to fill extremely large boots.

Six years on, I was walking down Dalston High Road with my friend Kiki who was sporting her new boots. Suddenly a grey Uno pulls over. Kiki starts conversating with the passenger and the driver gets out to speak with me, he liked my hair cut. He was a twenty-four, dark skin, gold teeth brother who walked with a high chest and cocky with it too. He had lyrics but so did I. He asked me for my number, and I agreed on one condition, he must remember it as I don't like writing down my number in public. He remembered it and he called me that same evening and that's when I came to know Daniel.

Slightly rough at the edges he had a tender side to him. It's funny how quick things can transpire particularly when you're not looking for it and then before you know it, you're calling it love. It happened quicker than I could calculate, I didn't have time to second guess my move, or talk myself out of it. Timing is everything and he caught me at the right time. My hardened exterior was melting whether I liked it or not.

Meeting Daniel had filled a void that evoked long since buried emotions and memories. I never planned for them to come out but when they did, I could not stop its flow, I didn't want too and for the first time in a long time, I was feeling again. Powerful forces were conjuring its magic releasing raw heart felt emotions that knew no inhibitions. Presented with an opportunity to grasp happiness, I went for it.

It lasted a non-conventional, highly eventful and testing nineteen years with three major breaks. Ultimately, we were like a ship out at sea with no real destination. We neither stopped to replenish or make repairs, we were adrift while our vessel was slowly rotting. Eventually that ship became a row boat. We lost the map, compass and ate the remaining supplies, all we had left was the oars. I was singing row, row, row your boat, but I never heard the echo of gently down the stream.

No coincidences there, at primary school when I would play kiss chase, I'd be running with the rest of the girls, screaming all excited but every so often, I would stop during the chase wanting to be caught only to realize, no one was actually chasing me, they were in fact running past me.

With rejection and disappointment as my rod and shield, unable to see my own part to play, I rebounded into another relationship. I remember saying to myself I would like to have a son before my daughter turns ten years old, or that's it, no more babies. I was even prepared to get married and commit, the full nine yards, stuff all this bouncing around. As quick as I had planted that seed of thought, within several months I fell pregnant and marriage was being put on the table.

The only problem was, I hadn't addressed or let go of my past hurt. The relationship was doomed to fail as quick as it had begun for, I hadn't entered with the mindset and heart of starting a new, I had entered with blocking longstanding pain and he too was the same. Driven by disappointment and blinded by old wounds, I ran into a love I thought I wanted only to find I didn't, yet the seed had already been sown, and the deed done. I got what I asked for, a child and a man who wanted to marry me and regardless of what decisions brought me there, I was there. All that was left for me to consider was, what next. Next time I'll be a bit more specific with what I ask for.

It was wasn't long before the hair line fractures began to appear. Before the year was out the relationship became turbulent, toxic and self-sabotaging, which caused a great strain upon my daughter. It too effected the relationship between my mother and I, and she stopped coming down to see me, likewise, so did my friends. I had worked so hard to get things on an even keel, my home was a home and for the best part as a family, we were happy. I messed up and invited someone in even more messed up than myself, I hadn't done my homework, I didn't learn my lessons. This time around I was determined that what I didn't learn when I was with Daniel, I was going to learn with this one. I was going to get my life back on track and take back my power, so I could once again recognize my reflection in the mirror and be a mum, a daughter and a woman I could be proud of.

Eight and a half months into the pregnancy the one thing I dreaded the most, the one bridge I dare not look at in fear I would have to cross it. The issue of our once beloved house resurfaced. It was falling apart at the seams, literally.

136

Not even a squatter would have wanted to stay there. The pigeons had somehow bought the top part of the house and invited in all their friends and family and when it rained the walls and ceilings created numerous mini waterfalls, picturesque for a magazine, but not when you live there. When you walked up the stairs you really did have to tread lightly, there had been previous cave ins. Once the ceiling under the stairs fell in missing Nicky by a margin. The feeling of the house being alive never left me and I was sure it wanted to take my mother with it, not on my watch.

It was going to be a tall order trying to get mum to do something she didn't want to do, naturally I hoped this time she would yield. Surveyors, Social Workers, Housing Officers, Psychiatrists, Police Officers all came with their note pads asking their rhetorical questions. Within a one-week period the house had been deemed unsafe to live in and mother would have to move. I must say she hated strangers in her home but with all the people coming in and out, she held her composure and remained quite passive. It made me question is she really mad or not?

The housing arranged several properties for us to look at for the following week. It wasn't easy, but I persuaded mum to view the properties and eventually we agreed upon a quaint little one bed room ground floor flat with a garden. It was local to the shops and familiar to her current surroundings. It was only a stone throw away from where she currently lived but, she had to move out by the following Wednesday or be forcibly removed. Mother signed all the papers but when she got back home, she stated to me "I'm not moving anywhere." I pleaded with her crying an ocean of tears to see sense. I screamed at the top of my lungs, "If they take you away then it's out of my hands, I can't protect you," but she didn't give rise to my weeping or whaling's.

Bewildered by her response, I considered the notion, is it possibly mother wanted to go. My desire to protect her was formed out of fear, disappointment and loss and as much as I wanted to protect her from outside forces, how had me holding onto this mindset helped her to develop, to fulfill her own needs? How had my actions shaped her to be as independent as she could be? Maybe in over protecting her, by holding on so tightly I had indeed held her back.

The deadline was up, and mother stood true to her word, she was not moving. I am now in my last week ready to give birth. They came to collect her on the Wednesday morning. I chose not to be there, I know it sounds selfish, but my spirit would not have been able to bare seeing her carted off. The thought of knowing my mother was going back into the hands of the mental health system where often you couldn't tell the patients from the doctors concerned me.

Later that afternoon I went to the house where the neighbor downstairs informed me mum went calmly and wasn't hand cuffed this time, that was a relief. When I finished with my thank you's and she went back into her home, I sat on the stairs outside my mother house and just cried. All I could do now, was plead her corner and pray someone would cling onto my words of love that I have for this woman and treat her accordingly.

By the Thursday morning I went into labour. With each pain I felt in the delivery suite, my thoughts went to my mother who was less than two hundred yards away from me in the hospital mental ward. By the early hours of the morning I had delivered a son. An eight-pound baby boy who I called CJ. He was born with his eyes open, just looking at me. I was slightly taken aback, I had to ask the nurse is that normal. Reassured I hadn't just given birth to Damion, I couldn't wait to hold my beautiful baby, I just had to wait for the pethidine to wear off.

The next day I had been discharged from hospital. My aunt Yvonne came to pick me up and with baby in hand we headed straight to the mental ward. When my daughter was born I took her to see my mum the next day and I was going to do the same with my son however, I was not allowed to enter into the ward with a newborn so, I just held CJ against the pane of glass behind the closed doors for a minute or two so she could clearly see him. As I walked away, I cried my heart out, the pain was unmeasurable.

It wasn't long before I attended the first meeting regarding my mum with the psychiatrists, key workers etc. There was about six of them and two of us. Mum sat beside me remaining quite calm. There seemed to be an air of indifference about her. The meeting started off good however, as the professional's questions became more intense, my fears soon turned into tears. The main psychiatrist chairing the meeting who looked like a patient asked me, "Why are you crying?" so I replied, "Because none of you know my mum. You sit here with your pens and note pads asking all sorts of scripted questions, taking notes and making judgments about someone's life based on a fifteen to twenty -minute meeting.

What can you possibly know about her, her strengths, how can you diagnose her and truly get it right when your assessment is screening for what she cannot do? I don't want her pumped with drugs and zombified like they did her before, no one was concerned about her so much so, that she walked out of hospital whilst under a section and no one questioned it. She's only here because of the house not because anyone was concerned about her welfare. This is my heart beat right here and whatever hurts her will hurt me and I don't want anyone to hurt my mum."

For that short moment in time I was that thirteen year-old girl once again, who had walked into social services seeking help.

He acknowledged my concerns and let me know my mum would be in good hands and that as her officially carer, any treatment advised would not be administered without my consent, naturally this made me feel better and I relaxed somewhat. The medication they gave mum seemed to balance her thoughts and noticeably our conversations were more fluent, comprehensive. For the first time I didn't have to decipher what she was trying to say.

Mum flourished in a way I couldn't have imagined. She was active within the ward, staff would often say to me when I came to visit her, "She's a good cook your mum." I do believe she was using the moment to rest but also to socialize. She never once complained or requested to leave, she found it amusing she had to be escorted to the shops.

Even though the atmosphere wasn't always healthy, there is no fun in seeing someone wrestled to the ground and injected but, mum was interacting with people. I could see the light in her face, the burden of the outside world seemed to disappear. I brought her fags, clothing, toiletries and gave her pocket money, mum was doing alright. She was receiving the things I couldn't give her, time, consistency and connections with others. I saw how it had made a difference in her communication, social interaction and general being, mum appeared happy.

Mother stayed at the hospital for several weeks. When the day came for her to leave there was a noticeable change in demeanor. I could feel the weight of her unspoken words, "I'm tired and I'm not sure if I want to do this anymore." Mum was entering a new cycle in her life after thirty years and I knew it wasn't going to easy for her. She had endured so many changes and challenges but to her credit she is a born fighter and I was proud of her.

Mother settled into her new environment quite well. She started taking charge over certain things for example putting money on the electric key or answering the mobile phone. I never thought in a million years that she would or could ever do this as simple as a task as it may seem. Whilst progress has come in small chunks with plenty back and forth, the lessons and learnings have been invaluable. Mum needed more than just me, and I needed to release the fear of the past mindset, so I too could heal.

Months later I received a message from the same psychiatrist who looked like a patient. He introduced a play writer to me regarding my story with my mum. That was the first time an attempt of creating a stage performance of my life was explored. Whilst it never manifested into fruition, it did open the doorway to start collecting my memories and the fact the psychiatrist thought of us, it told me there was a story in me to be told.

It was years later that my brother came to me in a vision which was the last time I remember seeing him. I was at my grans house, but it resembled more of a house in the clouds, everybody was coming in and out and that's when he made his presence known to me. I looked to the family to show them he was here, but they could not see him, that's when I knew he had come to speak with me. He had grown and matured, he looked so handsome with his beard. He wore a blue with silver undertone suit, it looked tailor made. All he came to tell me was he was crossing over and with that he walked off. I tried to stop him to ask more questions, but I couldn't find the words to say neither did I have the voice to speak them. All I could do was watch him walk off into the clouds. I knew he was alright, I knew he was at piece.

Through my mother's life transformations my life too had been transformed. I had come a long way from that little girl hitched up underneath her mother's skirt who played with dolls heads. I have loved and lost and lost and loved. I have learnt that everything happens for a reason and that there is always something to learn, where there's a will there is always a way.

My journey of recall has left me amazed and enthused to further share my imprinted collection of knowledge. I have crossed bridges of uncertainty and broken-down defenses that no longer serve their purpose. With gateways opened to communication and inner healing, I was finally recognizing I was my own artist creating the picture of my own future.

I had learnt about womanhood and relationships from watching the men and women in and outside of my life. Fraught with many choices and decisions, some I didn't want to make but never the less I had to take, I did a lot in its name sake. Not everything is black and white when you're fighting the war of the heart. Like scotch bonnet on my fingers which I forgot then rubbed into my own eyes, sometimes it stung, it burned, and I cried. Yet through it all I have loved in ways never known to me before, something I cannot regret for it has assisted me in finding the key that unlocks my own door.

Whether family, friends or partners I learnt that when I accepted that I am not responsible for other people's life decisions or choices, I can only choose to actively participate or not, I was able to see that everyone journey with its ups and downs, whether it makes sense to me or not are necessary for their own development to completing their true-life cycle. By continuously intervening or feeling somehow, I could make it right, or holding onto ideals long since passed that no longer serve the current time, I restricted my own experiences to have the relationships I truly wanted thus creating delays and false starts. When my awakening into acceptance took a hold of me, those first steps of stepping back was when I truly started moving forward.

Spiritually I am forever evolving to gain a higher understanding of being, feeling, and thinking about the many messages and visitations I have received and encountered over the years. It has truly shaped my mindset to see beyond the surface revealing the many layers and dimensions that exist within us all.

In my spiritual observatory I travel through space where time does not exist and am shown by the many messengers, guides, teachers and protectors the past, present and future. It has afforded me the insight to offer wisdom as well as relay warnings. It has taught me about the higher purpose I serve within the universe I live. I cannot buy a piece of mind I can only create it and when I have, when I have used those gifts given to me and acted in accordance to alignment, I have lived my best life.

When I walked into the light as a new mother, I also came to know the dark. A fine line so fragile in flesh yet unbreakable in spirit. From the moment of conception, carrying and delivery I came to know, What is sacrifice? What is being selfless? What is having strength? What is having courage? What is being responsible? What is a teacher? What is a protector? What is it to guide? What is a friend? What is a mother? What is love?

Once upon a time I thought my mum was the

weakest link, the burden I alone had to carry, the secret never to be told. However, with time and introspection like the rising of the sun, all that is, is revealed. My mum is and has always been my greatest strength, drive and inspiration. Through her mental illness I found compassion, patience, perseverance and a strength of character and spiritual growth. Imparted with courage, faith, belief, trust and self-love our relationship has been baptized and reborn so once again mother and daughter can become one.

.

L - #0067 - 300119 - C0 - 210/148/8 - PB - DID2427143